I'm Potty Training My Child

What NOW?

Proven Methods That Work

Patricia Wynne, PhD

Lesson Ladder
Success within reach!

www.lessonladder.com
21 Orient Avenue, Melrose, MA 02176

XAMonline, Inc., Cambridge, MA 02141
© 2013 by Sharon A. Wynne. (Text and illustrations)

Published 2013
Printed in the United States
1 2 3 4 5 6 7 13 12 11 10 09 08

Lesson Ladder: an imprint of XAMonline, Inc.
21 Orient Avenue
Melrose, MA 02176
Fax: 1-617-583-5552
Email: customerservice@lessonladder.com
Web: www.lessonladder.com

Text: Patricia Wynne
Contributing authors: Krista Beck and Elizabeth Heller

Illustrations by Valerie Bouthyette
Cover photos provided by www.canstockphoto.com: 6070519 © Can Stock Photo Inc./JIRKAEJC; 3022699 © Can Stock Photo Inc./ROBNROLL; 7964001 © Can Stock Photo Inc./ERIERIKA;

Library of Congress Catalog Card Number: (pending)

Wynne, Patricia.
  I'm Potty Training My Child: Proven Methods That Work

  150 pp., ill.
  1. Title 2. Toilet Training - Handbooks, Manuals, etc. 3. Infants - Handbooks, Manuals, etc. 4. Child Care - Handbooks, Manuals, etc.
  5. Children - Health and Hygiene - Handbooks, Manuals, etc.

  HQ770.5 W966 2012   649.62 W99 2012
  ISBN: 978-0-9848657-6-5

Contents

I'm
Potty Training
My Child

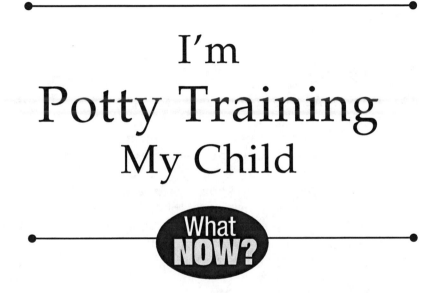

Introduction

Are You Ready?
You Can Do It!

CONGRATULATIONS! You've reached another milestone in your child's development: potty training! If you are like most parents, you have probably arrived at this new developmental stage with many different emotions, questions, and concerns. On the one hand, you are probably very excited about the idea of your child soon being out of diapers. At the same time, you may also be feeling confused and overwhelmed about how you are going to get from point A (diapers) to point B (dry underwear) with your patience and sanity intact. Where do you begin? How do you know when your child is ready? What's the best method for getting the job done? Now it's time to stop stressing, because *I'm Potty Training My Child: Proven Methods That Work* has got you covered!

HOW THIS BOOK WILL HELP YOU

Have no fear! There is no need to go it alone, or read thousands of pages of potty training manuals, or listen to the advice of well-meaning family and friends. You have chosen the perfect book to accompany and guide you on this new adventure! *I'm Potty Training My Child: Proven Methods That Work* gives you all the tools, information, and confidence you need to prepare for and achieve complete potty training success. This book will also enable you to proceed smoothly and patiently throughout the entire process. The information provided in these pages is succinct and clear, and contains many special elements to help you along. *Most importantly, this book asks you to keep your child's unique needs and personality in mind, and always, always proceed with patience and love.*

SPECIAL TEXT FEATURES

Each chapter in *I'm Potty Training My Child: Proven Methods That Work* is designed to guide you successfully through the potty training process. Along with the detailed information provided in each chapter, there are special features woven throughout the book that will support your efforts. These include handy checklists, pro and con charts, special tips, and brief vignettes from fellow parents. You can use these elements as you read along, or flip back and forth to them at any time to refresh your memory. Here's a brief description of each unique book feature.

"Parent Point-of-View" Quotes

Just like talking with a good friend, the Parent Point-of-View quotes sprinkled throughout this book will help you feel supported in your potty training process. Whatever situation you are facing, whatever emotion you may be experiencing, *rest assured* that hundreds of other parents have experienced that same thing. These brief parent stories let you know that you are not alone!

User-Friendly Charts and Quick Tips

The various charts within this book provide an easy and succinct way to evaluate your child's readiness, identify the supplies you might need, and determine whether or not your child will benefit from a reward system. You can use these features to help guide your decision making. Similarly, the "Quick Tips" boxes will help you keep key ideas and guidance in mind as you support your child on their potty training adventure.

Flexible Text Organization

This book is designed to be used in any way that best suits your needs. You can read the book chronologically from cover to cover, or turn to sections of particular interest in any order that you choose. You may wish to read all the charts in one sitting, or just peruse the Quick Tips and Parent Point-of-View quotes. However you choose to use this book, it will provide just the right support and guidance for your potty training journey.

BRIEF CHAPTER OVERVIEWS

Chapter 1: *Quick Summaries to Get You Started*, offers useful readiness checklists, and a supplies checklist. This is a great place to begin your journey and get a lay of the potty training land.

As you will learn in this book, two of the most important elements of successful potty training are a positive, patient attitude and honoring the unique needs and personality of your child. Chapter 2: *Setting the Right Tone with Your Child*, covers these key factors in detail and reminds parents how important it is to respect your child's development and potty train in a patient, positive manner.

One of the questions most frequently asked by parents is, "How do I know when my child is ready to potty train?" Chapter 3: *Is Your Child Ready? Are You?*, covers this question in depth, and includes a look at a child's emotional and physical readiness. Also covered are more practical and environmental considerations regarding potty training— including day care or preschool requirements, a second child on the way, and going green. By encouraging careful consideration, this chapter guides you in evaluating all the elements in your child's life that may or may not point to potty training readiness.

As you have begun to prepare for potty training, you may have noticed the vast array of potty training supplies available to assist you—everything from potty chairs and toilet toppers to potty training DVDs, books, and dolls. Chapter 4: *Your Potty Training Toolkit*, outlines the components of your potty training "toolkit", and helps you evaluate what items might work best for you. This chapter also covers potty charts that you can create to track your child's progress, as well as different motivational rewards for your child.

Before your child sits on the potty for the very first time, it is important to lay the groundwork for the toilet training adventure ahead. Chapter 5: *Pre-Potty Training with Your Child*, takes you step-by-step through the *pre-potty* training process which includes looking for your child's bodily clues and patterns, introducing your child to the potty, common potty vocabulary, motivating your child, and modeling the appropriate potty behavior for your child.

Chapter 6: *Potty Training: The Nuts and Bolts*, takes you through the actual potty training process step-by-step, and includes information on common challenges, important tips, and alternative potty training techniques. This chapter provides the *nuts and bolts* of potty training as outlined in the 13 Key Steps of Potty Training; this will prove invaluable to you and your child as you embark on this new adventure.

Potty training is rarely a linear process. Every child experiences accidents, setbacks, and even regressions along the way. Chapter 7: *Common Problems and Obstacles*, explains these common problems, and illuminates how they are a natural part of the potty training process. This chapter also provides encouragement and reminds you to be patient and accepting with your child when accidents do happen.

Chapter 8: *Special Situations*, offers guidance on handling special situations that often arise during the potty training process—including traveling, separated parents, using public restrooms, and sleepovers. This chapter also covers special situations such as raising children with special needs and how to handle unwanted advice.

Finally, Chapter 9: *Common Questions and Answers about Potty Training*, presents a summary of the most common questions that parents ask about the potty training process, and helpful answers to guide you through a variety of scenarios.

AN IMPORTANT MESSAGE FOR PARENTS

I'm Potty Training My Child: Proven Methods That Work is intended to be a valuable resource for you and your family as you make your way down the potty training path. *But remember: you are the one and only expert on your child.* You understand their temperament, what motivates them, what scares them, and how to best move them forward in their development. When you combine your unique knowledge of your child with the information in this book, you will have everything you need to make your potty training process a huge success!

Take a deep breath. Potty training is a time of *transition* for both you and your child. Up to this point, your child has relied on a diaper to pee and poop. It's a familiar and automatic process. Your child poops or pees, and you change their diaper. Now, though, you will be asking your child to radically change their behavior and thoughts about pooping and peeing, and your behavior and thoughts will have to change along with theirs. This shift in thinking is significant for everyone involved. *Everyone* (your child, spouse, grandparents, and caregivers) will need to adjust and transition.

Just remember: There is no rush. No hurry. No set deadline you and your child have to meet. Potty training takes time, and how much time depends solely on your child. Allow them the space and time to find their way, and you will find your way as well. Potty training can actually be a joyful time for both you and your child. When undertaken with the spirit of respect and teamwork, this adventure can also provide a special opportunity to deepen the bond that you and your child already share.

Have confidence! You can do this! Everyone can. Everyone does! We all learn to recognize the signs of needing to poop and pee, and we all learn to use a toilet. Your child will learn, too. The real question is: will you and your child get through potty training happily, or with angst and frustration? The choice is really yours. If you follow the guidance in this book, you will find that potty training can be a joyful, bonding, and even fun experience with your child. You are ready! Go ahead, begin your new adventure and let *I'm Potty Training My Child: Proven Methods That Work* show you the way!

1

Quick Summaries to Get You Started

Let's get started! This chapter provides quick summaries of some of the most important information found in later chapters. For extended and detailed coverage on any topic, please read the specific chapters that we reference with each checklist or summary.

READINESS CHECKLISTS

As you will learn in this book, the most important ingredient in successful potty training is your child's *readiness* to begin learning. There are certain physical and emotional milestones that children should meet before beginning the potty training experience. Understanding the relationship between these milestones and a child's ability to learn potty training is an important first step for parents. Please see the Physical Readiness and Emotional Readiness Checklists on the next few pages. If your checkmarks mostly appear in the "Yes" column, it is probably a good time to begin potty training with your child! For more detailed information about readiness and readiness milestones, please see Chapter 3: *Is Your Child Ready? Are You?*

Is My Child Ready?—Physical Milestones

The age ranges included here represent averages. All children develop at different rates. Consult with your pediatrician if you have concerns about your child's development.

Bladder Control	Average Age	YES	NO
Can stay dry for several hours at a time	18 - 30 months		
Urinates large quantities at a single time	About 24 months		
Stays dry all night	Usually 24 - 30 months		
Bowel Control	Average Age	YES	NO
Has well formed bowel movements	12 - 24 months		
Shows signs of impending bowel movements	Birth - 30 months		
Wants privacy during bowel movements	About 24 months, but may not happen at all		
Motor Skills	Average Age	YES	NO
Able to walk	10 - 18 months		
Able to run	18 - 24 months		
Able to pull pants up and down	18 - 24 months		
Able to take clothes off	18 - 24 months		
Able to put clothes on	24 - 30 months		
Able to wash hands alone	24 - 30 months		
Able to reach behind themselves to wipe	24 - 30 months		
Indicates need to go/informs parent of soiled diaper	18 - 30 months		

Go to www.lessonladder.com for a downloadable version of this checklist.

Is My Child Ready?—Emotional Milestones ✓

The age ranges included here represent averages. All children develop at different rates. Consult with your pediatrician if you have concerns about your child's development.

Emotional Skills	Average Age	YES	NO
Ability to follow simple directions	About 24 months		
Mimics the behavior of adults or older siblings	18 - 24 months		
Shows an interest in putting things away/putting things in place	18 - 24 months		
Begins to show interest in choosing own clothes	24 - 30 months		
Shows pride when accomplishing goals	18 - 30 months		
Begins to do things for him or herself—gets own toys, shows self-reliance	24 - 30 months		
Is willing to try new things	24 - 30 months		
Begins to be cooperative with others	About 30 months		
Begins to play alone/entertain oneself	18 - 30 months		
Does not like feeling of soiled diaper	18 - 30 months, though some children never feel this		
Shows interest in others using the toilet	18 - 30 months, though some never will show interest before potty training begins		

Go to www.lessonladder.com for a downloadable version of this checklist.

SUPPLIES CHECKLIST

There's no getting around the fact that you will need certain basic supplies in order to begin potty training with your child. The nice surprise, however, is that buying these supplies won't break the bank. You can also have a lot of fun picking out some of these items with your little one! For more information about each of these items, see Chapter 4: *Your Potty Training Toolkit.*

Once you've reviewed the checklist on the next page and decided what you do and don't need, take this list with you to the store to be sure that you don't forget anything.

Potty Training Supplies Checklist ☑

Necessary Items	Purchase Yes/No?	How Many?
Potty Chair		
Toilet Topper (portable seat)		
Training Pants		
Pull-ups		
Extra underwear and pants		
Footstool		
Travel or Emergency Kit		
• Diapers or pull-ups		
• Toilet topper		
• Wipes		
• Ointment		
• Full changes of clothing		
• Plastic bags		
Optional Items	Purchase Yes/No?	How Many?
Plastic Bed Sheets or Waterproof Pads		
Potty Training Doll		
Potty Training Children's Books		
Potty Chart		
Motivational Rewards (stickers, toys, candy)		
Diaper Liners		
Targets for the Toilet		
Pre-moistened Disposable Wipes		
Toddler Hygiene Supplies (soap, hand sanitizer)		

Go to www.lessonladder.com for a downloadable version of this checklist.

2

Setting the Right Tone
with Your Child

THE POWER OF PATIENCE

The potty training process can test the patience of even the most experienced parent. As adults, we tend to want things to unfold smoothly, according to our plans, with little deviation from our expectations. While all parents want to foster the beginnings of independence in their toddler, the toddler's and parent's expectations do not always align. Making the process of potty training a learning experience for your child, instead of a test of wills, can help shape the relationship you will have with your child for years to come. Just like all the other milestones we see our children achieve, teaching our children to use the potty can be an amazing bonding experience between parent and child. *The best way to support your child through this learning adventure is to stay focused on being supportive and patient.* This, of course, is easier said than done, but it is an essential ingredient for toileting success.

Remember that All Children are Different

While many children are able to quickly complete the potty training phase, often within a matter of weeks, others will take months or sometimes a few years to become *fully* potty trained. Each child learns at an individual pace, and some will take longer than others. It is important for parents to remember that this holds true for siblings as well. Just because your first child potty trained quickly does not mean that subsequent children will follow the exact same path. Each child is unique and approaches learning differently. Some children just naturally love the challenge of learning new things. They see their parents doing something interesting, and want to learn to do it too! Other children are seemingly uninterested in potty training, or even resistant. An important concept that we will cover in Chapter 3: *Is Your Child Ready? Are You?*, is determining whether or not your child is ready to begin the potty training process. Experience has shown that readiness is a key factor in successful potty training, and we will give you specific and helpful tips for determining whether or not your child is ready.

A NATURAL LEARNING PROCESS

As soon as children are born, they begin seeing adults and
older children using the toilet to go to the bathroom, and will
naturally want to do the same *when the time is right for them.*
Parents can begin talking to their babies about using the potty
as soon as it seems appropriate—usually around age one or
even earlier for some children who are more communicative.
Taking a child into the bathroom to show them the process is
not embarrassing at all for a child. Children are naturally
curious and want to know what their parents are doing and
why. Just as you explain your other routines and habits to your
child, you should talk to your child about why you go to the
bathroom and what you are doing. Beginning the process early
in the child's life by bringing them into the bathroom and
showing them that using the toilet is natural can help
tremendously when the time is right to begin potty training.
Every living creature pees and poops; it is important that we
clearly convey to our children that this natural process is not
something shameful. People say "nature's calling!" for a
reason!

However, if you are uncomfortable bringing your child
into the bathroom with you, you can use a children's book to
talk to your child about peeing and pooping on the potty—
such as *Sophie's Magic Underwear* written by Kristin Kroha.
You can use the illustrations to talk to your child about the
process of going to the bathroom, what you do when you use
the potty, and why. *The key is to be positive and comfortable
when talking with your child, so choose the method of
illustration that works best for you.*

A POSITIVE APPROACH

The onset of toddlerhood and a child's newfound independence can be frustrating at times for parents. Children begin to discover that they have power over their own bodies, actions, and words, and they begin to test the limits of each. Any parent who has scrambled after their running toddler or had a contest of wills over what outfit to wear knows that a natural part of toddlerhood is emerging independence. Despite these challenges, *maintaining a positive and encouraging tone in your communication with your toddler is so very important to the potty training process*. It shows the child that you are an active partner on their path towards independence, and that you support them in learning new things and facing new challenges. A young toddler may not understand every single word we say, but they certainly understand our tone.

Some children will be eager to begin potty training, especially if they've been involved in choosing their own potty chair or choosing story books about potty training that are interesting to them. Other children may not seem at all interested, which may or may not be a sign that they are not yet ready. It is important for parents to be able to read their child and determine if the lack of interest is really a sign that the child isn't ready, or if this is just the child's normal disposition. It can be beneficial to begin introducing the concepts of potty training at around age two to two-and-a-half, even if the child shows no interest. It is also important to introduce the idea in a positive way.

Regardless of when the potty training process begins, parents should take a positive or matter-of-fact approach with the child instead of a negative or punitive approach. Negativity and the process of potty training never mix well, and can cause the process to be delayed for months as the child asserts their will over yours. Parents need to remember that children control their own bodies and make their own choices about whether or not they will use the potty. Use of a negative or critical approach to potty training can cause the child to shut down emotionally or reject potty training altogether.

Parent Point-of-View

"One day during potty training with my son, I was super tired and had a bad cold. He sat down on his potty chair and peed—which I praised him for. He insisted on sitting longer to try to poop. We read books, listened to music, and chatted. After fifteen minutes, I was losing my patience. I tried to cajole him off the potty but he wouldn't budge. Eventually, I insisted that he get up and he picked up the potty and dumped his pee all over the bathroom floor. Not only did I have a job cleaning up, it took a month to get him to sit on the potty chair to poop again. I never lost my patience after that. No matter what, stay positive!"

The Importance of Praise

A positive approach to potty training will include plenty of praise for your child. All children seek the praise of their parents and respond positively to it. At the beginning of potty training, children should be commended for even the smallest of victories. It is helpful for parents to point out exactly what they are praising. Phrases like "Great job!" are helpful for beginning potty trainers, but it is even more helpful for parents to be *specific* about what was great. A better phrase might be, "You sat down on your potty chair! Great job!" The child will know exactly which action earned the praise, and will therefore be more likely to repeat it. It is also beneficial to praise a child's efforts, and not just the positive outcome. For example, you can praise your child for working hard on potty training and following your directions.

Quick Tip: Be Positive!
A negative or critical approach can cause your child to shut down emotionally, or reject potty training altogether.

Some parents do not feel comfortable doling out praise for the potty training process. While it is not necessary to commend the child for doing a basic task, parents can still point out what the child is doing and let them know that they are doing it correctly. For example, the parent could simply state, "You sat down on your potty chair." Being matter-of-fact is also helpful for children who have been participating in the potty training process for some time (after the small victories have been celebrated multiple times). Parents should continue to point out that the behavior is correct, even if they do not feel that it is appropriate for praise. Remember all your great teachers? This is exactly what they did; they made sure their feedback clearly communicated what you did well so that you would know what to continue doing!

The key take-away message is that *negativity should not be used in potty training*. Even in the most frustrating of times (of which there will be many), it is more beneficial to the child, the parent, and the process to refrain from criticism. It is better to say nothing or delay potty training for a time than it is to punish a child for an accident or "not doing it right." Potty training is a very personal matter for children, and one of their first lessons in true independence. Parents that yell, become frustrated, punish, or discipline toddlers because of potty training issues will find that they may have a child in diapers well into preschool or even beyond.

A CHALLENGING ADVENTURE

The parent that embarks on the potty training journey with a positive attitude, and who sees the process as an adventure is more likely to be successful helping their child to learn. Toddlerhood brings many challenges for parents and children, potty training among them. It is helpful for parents to figure out early in the process how they can remain calm and positive, even in the face of great frustration. Before you begin potty training, create a "Patience Plan" for yourself. Some parents find deep breathing or yoga works for calming frayed nerves, while others need to take a walk or jog to get the feelings out of their system. We will discuss this concept in greater detail in Chapter 6: *Potty Training: The Nuts and Bolts!*

Understand that while this is a frustrating time for almost all parents, it does pass, and your abilities as a parent will improve based upon this experience. Keeping a positive, kind, and gentle attitude with your child during potty training and the toddler years will show your child that they can trust you. It will also strengthen your parent-child relationship.

Quick Tip: The Power of Patience
Parents that yell, punish, or discipline their child during potty training will find that these tactics don't often yield positive results.

3

Is Your Child Ready? Are You?

As we explained in Chapter 2: *Setting the Right Tone with Your Child*, the decision of when to start potty training is different for each child. There are many valid reasons for parents to feel the need to begin potty training, but the parents' desires and the needs of the child should meet somewhere in the middle. It will only cause frustration and upset if the process is begun too early, or at a time that is not right for either or both of you. The time may seem right for you as the parent, but if your child is not developmentally, emotionally, or physically ready, potty training success will be delayed. Let's take a closer look at what usually spurs parents and caregivers to begin the potty training process.

COMMON REASONS TO BEGIN POTTY TRAINING

Parents have many different reasons for feeling the need to begin potty training with their child. Some reasons have less to do with the child and their developmental readiness, and more to do with outside pressures faced by parents. The truth is that sometimes the circumstances of our everyday lives dictate that we need to at least *begin* the potty training process with our toddler—even if it is earlier than we would prefer. These outside factors should be given consideration when making the decision to potty train, but they should be balanced by the readiness of your child.

The most common reason to begin potty training is straightforward and simple: age. As most children approach two years of age, it becomes apparent that they are becoming more physically and emotionally ready to begin learning about the potty. Other reasons are less about the readiness of the child—such as the need to transition your child into daycare, or the need to save money by not buying diapers.

Parent Point-of-View

"I vividly remember going to the park and listening to moms talk about where their child was in terms of potty training like it was a heated Olympic competition. While they quibbled back and forth about which child was more brilliant at aiming their pee at Cheerios in the toilet bowl, I vowed to resist the temptation to push my son into training before he was ready. It wasn't easy—I wanted him to be brilliant at peeing on Cheerios too—but I knew that waiting was the right thing to do for both of us!"

A Question of Age

Children are usually not ready to potty train before the age of two. Parents often begin thinking about potty training as this age approaches because they can see glimpses of interest and readiness in their child. Around this age, a child might start to ask questions about using the toilet, or begin to express discomfort and dissatisfaction with having to wear a wet diaper. Some parents feel that between two to three years of age is an appropriate time to begin potty training in earnest to help the child become more independent. It is also around age two that children begin to be physically capable of holding larger amounts of urine for longer periods of time, and the age where children begin to have more control over their bowel functions. These are two critical milestones of physical readiness that we will discuss in more detail later.

Daycare or Preschool Requirements

Many daycares, camps, and preschools have rules about children being fully potty-trained before being allowed to enroll. With this very common requirement in place, many parents feel a significant amount of pressure to begin potty training so that their child can attend the daycare or preschool of the family's choice. One can certainly understand why many daycares and preschools have this no-diapers policy. Some child care providers find it difficult to handle a dozen toddlers in diapers at once, or be responsible for potty training children who are all learning with slightly different techniques and reward systems. It can be quite a logistical challenge! For working parents, this no-diapers policy can have real implications. Many parents don't have the choice of staying at home with their toddlers who are not yet potty trained. They need to do what they can to make their toddler ready for preschool, even if this means potty training before the child is one hundred percent ready.

Parent Point-of-View
"I didn't want to start potty training so early, but I had to due to my daughter's daycare requirements. What worked for me was remaining positive and calm during the process even though I felt a tremendous amount of pressure to get my daughter out of diapers. I know for a fact that if I'd let the pressure get to me, it would have taken much longer to train her. In the end, it was a bonding experience for us and everything worked out in time!"

"Peer" Pressure

It is not uncommon to hear friends and family members make comments about the need for you to begin potty training with your child. The comments made by others can be very pointed at times, and may make you feel the need to move faster than you or your child would like. You may see other children around the same age beginning to potty train and feel like your child is lagging behind them. Your friends or family may make comments about how long your child has been in diapers, and attempt to nudge you to begin potty training. They may also boast that their own child is way ahead of yours developmentally. Who hasn't seen someone raise an eyebrow at a child they feel should be out of diapers already, and who hasn't been on the receiving end of unwanted parenting advice? *While these comments can make you doubt yourself, you know your child better than anyone, and you should begin potty training when you feel your child is ready.* Just like all other aspects of parenting, these decisions belong to you, not the peanut gallery.

> ***Quick Tip: Ready or Not?***
> While the time may seem right for you, if your child is not showing signs of readiness, success will be almost certainly be delayed.

Dollars and Cents

There is no question that diapers are expensive, and that ending this part of your child's babyhood would be a welcome addition to your pocketbook. You may have a genuine financial need to save the money that diapers cost, or you may just be looking forward to having more latitude in your family budget. Whether you use disposable diapers, cloth diapers, or some combination of both, we all know that having a young child can be costly. Once your child is potty trained, there will be one less expense each week. This is certainly something to look forward to—regardless of your specific financial situation!

The Stork is Coming

Having one child in diapers is hard work. If you have another baby on the way, you may want to potty train the oldest child so that you only have one child in diapers at a time. Not only is it expensive to have more than one child in diapers, many parents find it challenging to care for a newborn and also have to change the diapers of a toddler.

Another consideration is that potty training is a focused learning process, and is best done when you can give all of your attention to your toddler. Most parents would find it challenging to potty train a toddler and simultaneously care for a newborn. If possible, there are many benefits to getting the toddler's potty training process finished before bringing your new baby home. Potty training is also likely to be a more peaceful, rewarding, and successful adventure if you are not juggling multiple priorities at once. It is certainly possible to potty train your toddler while caring for a newborn, and many parents have done so successfully. That said, there are definite advantages to finishing the potty training process before coming home with a new baby.

Sensitive Skin

If your child has sensitive skin, diapers have probably been compounding the problem ever since birth. Potty training will mean the end of diaper rashes and a new sense of comfort for your child. While not every child experiences skin issues, it is not an uncommon problem by any means. If your child has been dealing with sensitive skin issues, you will no doubt love the opportunity to remove this daily discomfort from their lives!

Going Green

Most parents realize that the small steps they take in their own household can have a profound positive effect when combined with many other individuals taking action. The truth is that disposable diapers add millions of tons of waste to landfills each and every year. By potty training your child as soon as they are ready, a parent has the opportunity to do their part to help the environment. If the average toddler goes through 6 diapers a day, that means 2190 less diapers a year going into the trash from your household alone! For parents who are serious about environmental issues, it can be extremely satisfying to shorten the number of months or years their children are dependent on diapers.

> ***Parent Point-of-View***
> "There is so much pressure on parents these days in so many areas, including being green. When it came to the question of disposable diapers vs. forcing my daughter into underpants, I didn't know what to do until my mother said to me: 'It's a limited time no matter what you do, but do what is easiest. If it's disposable diapers, be sure to put extra effort into recycling other items in your household. If it's underpants, you'll be doing a lot of washing so be sure to save water elsewhere wherever you can. In the end, it will all even out.' What a relief! Don't get caught up in what society thinks you should do—do what's best for you and your family. That's the greenest thing you can do! I decided not to push it, use the diapers, and keep recycling elsewhere."

CHILD READINESS TO POTTY TRAIN

Let us now return to this very important issue of readiness. As we've already explained, children need to meet certain physical and emotional milestones before they are truly ready to start potty training. Ages of readiness are different for each child, and some children may reach milestones sooner than others. Let's take this opportunity to discuss the various components of "readiness" in greater detail.

Physical Readiness

There are many physical milestones that should be reached by a child before potty training is even contemplated. For example, children should be able to sit and stand, which usually happens early in toddlerhood, and they need to have achieved a certain amount of control over their own bodily functions. Until a child has reached these and other milestones, they are not ready to be fully potty trained. This makes perfect sense when you think about it carefully. In order to successfully potty train, a child has to be aware of when they need to pee or poop so that they can get to the potty before they wet or soil themselves. They need to be able to pull down their pants and sit on the potty. They need to be able to wipe themselves, get up from the potty, and wash their own hands. If a child hasn't progressed past crawling, they are simply not ready to take on the physical tasks that come along with using a potty. Let's look at some more of the key physical milestones in greater detail.

Bladder Control

The bladder of a two year old child is very small, holding only about three to four ounces of urine. The bladder grows as the child grows, increasing in its capacity by about one ounce every six months or so. The bladder is controlled by a small sphincter (or muscle) at the opening, also known as the urethra. For the child to be able to control their bladder, it is essential for them to gain control over this sphincter muscle—

which usually occurs at around age two to two-and-a-half. As your child gains more and more control over their bladder, you may notice they are able to stay dry for longer and longer periods of time and need changing less often. They may even be able to stay dry all night. This ability to "hold" urine for longer lengths of time is a good sign that your child may be ready to potty train.

Parent Point-of-View

"Potty training is a big transitional milestone for children and it needs to be approached thoughtfully, just like other life transitions. No one just wakes up one morning and says, 'We're moving to New Mexico today.' And no one should just wake up and say 'I think I'll start potty training today.' It takes planning and emotional, physical, and practical preparation. If you take the time and energy to be prepared, everything will go much more smoothly."

Important Facts about Bowel Control

Stool is formed in the intestine and held in the rectum by two small sphincters until there is enough pressure from the stool to have a bowel movement. When your child is a baby, they will poop any time there is even a small amount of pressure from stool. Over time, toddlers become more aware of the pressure put on these sphincters and learn what it feels like when they need to go. It is for this reason that potty training for poop often occurs before potty training for pee. The pressure felt when it is time to go poop is more obvious to them, and you may notice signs that they have indeed become aware of their need to go. However, as we've said before, the potty process is different for every child and you should not force your child one way or another. Whether they want to pee on the potty and poop in their diaper or vice versa, support their efforts and encourage their progress. Toddlers may begin hiding or going to a favorite spot when it is time to poop. You may also notice that they grunt or make a particular facial expression either before or during their bowel movements.

Children may also begin to have a bowel movement with some regularity, which gives you the opportunity to help them to the potty when you know it is around the time they normally need to poop.

Children usually have the ability to achieve bowel control about the same time as they achieve the ability to control their urine—between the ages of two and two-and-a-half. It is also around this time that bowel movements become better formed, giving the child the ability to wait until they are able to get to the toilet before soiling themselves, which can't happen with loose stool or diarrhea.

During the process of potty training, the child will learn which muscles need to be used to help push the poop out. Many of these muscles are the same muscles that are used to pee, which may help the child learn to pee and poop at the same time while using the potty. With practice, the child will learn which muscles need to be relaxed and which muscles need to be contracted in order to do one or the other.

Parent Point-of-View

"I had been pushing potty training every few months from the time my son could walk. I found the process very aggravating and stressful. One day, after a bath, he went upstairs and was naked as usual. I was downstairs tending to my newborn and thought I should go check on him before he had an accident. When I got to the top of the stairs, he was sitting on his potty. He said, "Mommy, Collin is pooping. Go back downstairs." I'm not sure if pushing him helped or not, but in retrospect it was so obvious when he was ready. I kind of wish that I had waited a little longer and focused solely on more passive pre-potty training techniques like reading children's books with him."

The Ability to Cooperate

Cooperative behavior and cooperative interactions with parents, family members, child care providers, and peers may also be signs of readiness. A child's ability to cooperate with others comes at different times for different children, but it is definitely a sign that they can follow directions and want to be helpful. For parents who are teaching their child to use the potty, this willingness to cooperate is extremely helpful. A defiant or resistant attitude means a lower chance of achieving a *smooth* transition to these new skill-sets. Like any other situation in life, the ability to cooperate is an important ingredient for success!

Communicating Discomfort with a Soiled Diaper

Another important readiness signal is when your child is able to tell you about their wet or soiled diaper. Children in late toddlerhood begin to dislike the feeling of a soiled diaper, and will often take it off themselves or ask a parent for help. This may be one of the most important milestones to be reached before beginning potty training. The child's ability to communicate that they are soiled shows that they know what is going on, and they want to do something about it!

Motor Skills

Toddlers achieve a number of physical and motor milestones in the second year of life, many of which are necessary for success in potty training. As stated before, children need the basic ability to stand up, walk, and sit down, all of which should be achieved sometime early in the second year. Children also need to be able to pull their pants up and down to be able to get to the potty in time. Since it is important to teach children about proper hygiene early, it is also necessary that the child be able to wash their own hands in the sink with soap and water. Wiping is another important part of the potty training process, and while children may need help with wiping for several years after initially potty training, it is vital that they begin learning the process early. Children should be able to reach behind themselves to at least attempt to wipe after using the potty.

Emotional Readiness

As we explained earlier, the emotional readiness of a child is just as important to the process of potty training as physical readiness. While some children reach the necessary physical and emotional milestones right on schedule, others may take several additional months. At the end of this chapter, we have repeated the Readiness Checklists from Chapter 1: *Quick Summaries to Get You Started*, for your easy reference. A review of these milestones will quickly give you an idea of whether or not it is a good time to start the training process, or if it would be best to wait a few more months. Toddlers develop very quickly and sometimes waiting a short period of time can be incredibly helpful.

The Ability to Follow Simple Directions

An important milestone that should be reached by a child before attempting potty training is the ability to follow basic and simple directions from an adult. (For example: "Bring me your sippy cup.") Due to developmental variations, some children may take longer to acquire this skill of processing simple spoken language and executing a simple request. If a child is not yet able to follow basic directions from an adult, or is particularly stubborn and refuses to follow directions, it can be very difficult to begin the process of potty training. Learning how to use the potty is not just learning *one* thing; it is learning an entire set and sequence of new skills. If a child isn't yet able or willing to follow simple directions, it will be very difficult to teach them all of the new things they need to learn in order to take this giant step towards becoming a big boy or girl. Of course, if you have any concerns about your child's inability to follow simple directions, please check with your pediatrician.

An Interest in Mimicking Adults

At a certain point in their young lives, toddlers begin to show an interest in trying to do the same things that adults do. We've all seen toddlers holding our cell phones to their ears and pretending to have an important conversation, or copying the way we sit or stand. This interest in mimicking adults or older siblings is an important signal that a child may be ready to begin potty training. While it may be many months before they are *physically* capable of using the potty, learning to sit on a potty chair *like mom and dad* can help the process in the long run and prepare the child for what is to come. One important part of potty training is the child's motivation to move on from being a "baby" to being a "big girl" or a "big boy", but they have to be emotionally mature enough to find this transition an exciting prospect. Parents should pay attention to whether or not their child is showing an interest in what goes on in the bathroom. As we explained earlier, allowing your toddler to accompany you on trips to the bathroom (to show them what happens when an adult or older sibling uses the toilet) can foster interest in the potty training process.

> **Parent Point-of-View** 🔍
> "My daughter began to play potty with her dolls. She would set up a scene for a tea party, have four of her dolls drink tea, and then have them fight over who was going to pee on the potty first. That's when I knew she was ready. Eventually, we moved the tea party into the bathroom and within a few weeks, my daughter was using the potty herself."

Signs of Emerging Independence

Another sign that a child is emotionally ready to start potty training is their interest in putting things away, or in choosing their own clothing. For much of early toddlerhood, children just wear what we pick out for them each day, or put their toys away where we say they should go. But as children start to gain a sense of independence, they want to start making these choices for themselves. They start to have an emerging idea of what they want, and how they want things to be. When your child begins showing that they are able to (and want to) make their own choices, this demonstrates that they are becoming more independent.

Emerging independence also shows itself in the form of being able to self-entertain, or play alone. They begin to not need someone there every moment to stimulate or entertain them—they can begin to rely on themselves for that! Independence is an important part of potty readiness because children need to be able to make the decision to use the potty. No matter what we want as parents, *the child has to actually decide that they want to use the potty*. As stated previously, the early stages of toddler independence generally begin late in the second year or early in the third.

The Willingness to Try New Things

Children nearing potty training readiness will also be open to trying new things. When children are excited about going new places, trying new foods, and meeting new people, it is an important indication that the child may be ready to try using the potty. When a child is fearful or going through big changes in their routine, such as starting a new daycare or welcoming a new sibling, it is often not the best time to start potty training.

It is important that parents understand that milestones are reached at different times for different children. While some children may be ready to begin potty training (or even be successfully potty trained) by age two, many others will need to wait several more months before the process can even begin. *We can't stress enough that there is a wide variety of 'normal' when it comes to the ability to potty train successfully, and that each child will achieve success in their own timeframe.*

> **Quick Tip: Ready or Not?** 💡
> When your child tells you that their diaper is wet, it is an important signal that they may be ready to begin potty training.

READINESS CHECKLISTS

We shared these same checklists with you in Chapter 1: *Quick Summaries to Get You Started*, but have included them again in this chapter for your easy reference. Keep in mind that the milestones listed on the next few pages represent *averages*. Ages of readiness differ for each child, and some children may reach specific milestones well ahead or somewhat behind what is considered "normal." If you have any concerns or questions about your own child's milestones or stages of development, please consult your pediatrician.

Note: Your child does not have to meet ALL the signs of readiness in order to begin potty training. However, if you check off the majority of boxes on the next few pages, that's a pretty good sign that your child is ready to start trying!

Is My Child Ready?—Physical Milestones ☑

The age ranges included here represent averages. All children develop at different rates. Consult with your pediatrician if you have concerns about your child's development.

Bladder Control	Average Age	YES	NO
Can stay dry for several hours at a time	18 - 30 months		
Urinates large quantities at a single time	About 24 months		
Stays dry all night	Usually 24 - 30 months		
Bowel Control	Average Age	YES	NO
Has well formed bowel movements	12 - 24 months		
Shows signs of impending bowel movements	Birth – 30 months		
Wants privacy during bowel movements	About 24 months, but may not happen at all		
Motor Skills	Average Age	YES	NO
Able to walk	10 - 18 months		
Able to run	18 - 24 months		
Able to pull pants up and down	18 - 24 months		
Able to take clothes off	18 - 24 months		
Able to put clothes on	24 - 30 months		
Able to wash hands alone	24 - 30 months		
Able to reach behind themselves to wipe	24 - 30 months		
Indicates need to go/informs parent of soiled diaper	18 - 30 months		

Go to www.lessonladder.com for a downloadable version of this checklist.

Is My Child Ready?—Emotional Milestones

The age ranges included here represent averages. All children develop at different rates. Consult with your pediatrician if you have concerns about your child's development.

Emotional Skills	Average Age	YES	NO
Ability to follow simple directions	About 24 months		
Mimics the behavior of adults or older siblings	18 - 24 months		
Shows an interest in putting things away/putting things in place	18 - 24 months		
Begins to show interest in choosing own clothes	24 - 30 months		
Shows pride when accomplishing goals	18 - 30 months		
Begins to do things for him or herself—gets own toys, shows self-reliance	24 - 30 months		
Is willing to try new things	24 - 30 months		
Begins to be cooperative with others	About 30 months		
Begins to play alone/entertain oneself	18 - 30 months		
Does not like feeling of soiled diaper	18 - 30 months, though some children never feel this		
Shows interest in others using the toilet	18 - 30 months, though some never will show interest before potty training begins		

Go to www.lessonladder.com for a downloadable version of this checklist.

4

Your Potty Training Toolkit

This chapter will help you make you make good decisions about the most important potty training items to buy. As you can probably guess, parents are bombarded with an almost endless number of potty training supplies available for purchase. There are many different types and styles of potty chairs, toilet toppers, training pants, and pull-ups. There are even fun accessories such as potty books and potty dolls. While many potty training items seem like necessities, *the only things that are truly required for potty training are a willing child, a patient parent, and a potty of some kind!*

Potty training supplies are readily available for purchase in many different types of stores and through online retailers. Most "big box" stores such as Wal-Mart and Target offer all of the supplies that parents need to start potty training, as do most child-oriented department stores. Supplies are readily available in most areas and should not be too hard to find. Basic supplies like a potty chair, toilet topper, toddler wipes, training pants, and a footstool can be purchased for a very reasonable price. (Of course, prices will increase depending upon the different accessories and extras that you buy.)

Let's take a look at some of the key potty training supplies that are available, talk about their basic features, and figure out the best choices for your specific needs. At the end of this section, we have also included a Supplies Checklist that summarizes the information in this chapter.

POTTY CHAIRS

Most people are already familiar with potty chairs, but we'll provide a quick overview just in case. A potty chair is a small, kid sized toilet that parents usually place in the bathroom next to the adult toilet. They are usually made of plastic and come in bright, child-friendly colors. As you might imagine, it can be difficult and scary for a young toddler to climb up onto an adult sized toilet. It is even more difficult for young children to hold themselves up on the toilet and not fall into the water! For these reasons, many parents choose to purchase a potty chair in order to begin potty training with their child. There are many different choices available for families who are in the market to buy a potty chair. It is even possible to get potty chairs emblazoned with some of the most popular children's cartoon characters like Dora the Explorer or Thomas the Train. Kids often like this personal and fun connection to their new potty.

Get Your Child's "Buy-In"

If you can, take your child with you when shopping for a potty chair. By allowing your child to choose a chair that they like in a favorite color or with a favorite character, it can make the process less intimidating and more exciting. This can also help with the transition to being a "big kid," and allow them to feel like they have a say in the process.

Key Features of a Potty Chair

The potty chair you choose should have a <u>wide enough base</u>
and be sturdy enough to not tip over when the child sits or
stands on it. Some potty chairs convert to a foot stool or a toilet
topper which can help your child with the later transition to
using an adult toilet. Many potty chairs have a <u>splash guard</u> to
help minimize accidental splashes during urination. If the
potty chair you choose includes a splash guard, be sure that it
is removable or low enough so that your child does not bump
themselves on it while sitting down. Bumps in this area can be
shocking to young children and may delay the process of potty
training.

    <u>Potty chair seats</u> will either be cushioned or hard. Some
children may prefer to have a cushioned seat since it is more
comfortable than a hard seat. Other children will have no
preference at all. If the chair does have a cushioned seat, choose
one with a sturdy, non-porous plastic covering so that it does
not absorb urine and begin to smell. Above all, remember to
choose a chair that your child likes and is excited about!

    Most importantly, potty chairs should be easy to clean.
All potty chairs require that the waste be collected in some type
of <u>bowl</u> that is emptied into the toilet after each use. Having a
bowl that is easily accessible for removal and cleaning is an
important factor in potty chair selection. In fact, some parents
encourage their children to empty their own waste into the
toilet early on in the potty training process. In their opinion,
this helps children learn where the waste goes after they are
done using the chair. On the other hand, many parents don't
want to deal with the potential mess or germs that might come
as a result of their child emptying their own potty chair.

There are many other features that can be included with potty chairs that may or may not be helpful for your child. For instance, some potty chairs are musical—they play a tune when wet. This can be fun for some children and scary for others. It can also interrupt the process and cause the child to stop what they are doing when they hear the music, or even stand up during the event. Other potty chair features may include arm rests, cartoon characters, and different styles or forms for the body of the chair. Deciding which features are most important for your child, and considering what they will find the most "inspiring" is the best way to choose the right seat for your toddler. If you have any concerns regarding your budget for buying a chair, you can pre-select chairs in your price range and only show your child those specific choices.

Potty Chair Pros and Cons

Some advantages to beginning potty training with a potty chair (as opposed to the regular "big" toilet) include the child friendliness of the product. Many children are excited to have something to use that is just for them and just the right size! Potty chairs are also less intimidating—especially for younger children. Some disadvantages of potty chairs include having to empty the waste after each use, and the need to later transition to the regular, adult sized toilet. (This is why some parents choose to start potty training on the big toilet from the get-go.)

Regardless of whether or not the child is lifted on and off the toilet by an adult, a footstool is still an important potty training item. When a child needs to poop, they can push down on the footstool with their feet. This helps them to use the muscles that are necessary for pooping on the toilet.

> **Parent Point-of-View**
> "I think having an extra potty is essential for play dates with other children who are in the potty training process. My son had a long and embarrassing meltdown the first time his friend came over and needed to pee and needed to use his potty. After the incident, we went out together and chose a 'play date potty.' Now everyone is happy."

Some Favorite Toppers

Most parents purchase at least one toilet topper to take with them on outings. The most popular model of toilet topper is the folding variety. This toilet topper folds up easily and can be carried in a diaper bag. Other parents prefer a fit-in model of toilet topper that actually fits in the opening of the adult toilet seat. The most popular of these has handles on the side, a splash guard, and comes in a variety of colors and patterns. Some of the fit-in models also have Disney or other cartoon characters printed on the seat which many children love. There are a wide variety of other types of toilet toppers, some with cushiony seats and some that merely make the opening of the toilet seat smaller for the child. Toilet toppers can range in price depending on the make and model.

On the next page, we have included a handy summary table that outlines the pros and cons of potty chairs and toilet toppers. We hope that you find this a helpful tool in your decision making!

POTTY CHAIRS VERSUS TOILET TOPPERS

Potty Chairs: Pros and Cons	
Pros	Cons
Child sized	The child may need to relearn some skills when it is time to move to the "grown up" toilet
Can be moved around inside the house	Difficult to take on the go
Child can choose their own chair based on favorite colors or characters	Not as realistic as using a "real" toilet
Toilet Toppers: Pros and Cons	
Pros	Cons
Child starts out using the "big" toilet	Child needs to be lifted onto or climb onto the toilet
Can be taken anywhere with the child	May need to purchase one for each toilet in the house
Realistic; much like using a real toilet	Not as many choices available for favorite colors or characters

TRAINING PANTS

You've probably heard about training pants from your parents or grandparents since these were used for potty training in their day. Training pants are washable and have thick, cloth middles to absorb accidents, but they are usually not waterproof and may require use of accompanying plastic pants. The main benefit of using washable training pants (as opposed to pull-ups) is that the child can really feel when they are wet. These do not lock away moisture like disposable diapers and pull-ups, and the child is immediately aware of the soggy and wet feeling!

Training pants also offer children an intermediate step to wearing underwear. Many parents buy several pairs of training pants with the intention of throwing them away when they are no longer needed, and then buy regular underwear after their child has experienced some potty success. Many children will enjoy choosing their own "big kid" underwear to wear after they are able to use the potty without accidents.

One disadvantage of using training pants is the frequent need to launder them. Children will have accidents, and parents may need several pairs of training pants per day to prevent the need for multiple launderings in a day. Parents that do not own a washing machine may instead want to use special pull-ups that have the added feature of allowing a child to really feel when they are wet.

Parent Point-of-View

"It was a mistake for us to use pull-ups with our toddler. He didn't really get the idea of potty training until we put him in big boy underwear. He did great all summer long. But when it came time for preschool to start that fall, we got nervous and had him wear pull-ups instead. He went right back to using the pull-ups like a diaper and we had to start potty training all over again. It didn't take as long the second time around, but we sure wished we'd trusted the process in the first place!"

PULL-UPS

Pull-ups are highly marketed to parents of toddlers for use during potty training. Almost every company that makes regular diapers makes a line of pull-ups, too. These usually have familiar cartoon characters printed on them and additional features built in to help children feel when they are wet. That said, many children cannot tell the difference between a pull-up and a disposable diaper, which is why many parents still opt for "old fashioned" training pants. Since pull-ups are so similar to diapers, another consideration is that some children will not want to wear what they view as a diaper after they have begun the potty training process. They may be more interested in wearing training pants or underwear to mimic their parents or older siblings.

Pull-ups can be useful for nighttime when children who are wearing underwear or training pants during the day do not want to have to go back into a "baby" diaper at night. Children should remove their pull-up shortly after waking to help them learn to use the potty first thing after getting up.

On the next page is a handy table that summarizes the pros and cons of pull-ups and training pants. We hope you find this tool helpful in your potty training decision process!

PULL-UPS VERSUS TRAINING PANTS

Pull-Ups: Pros and Cons	
Pros	Cons
Disposable	Adds waste to landfills
Easy to clean up	Child may not feel any difference between diaper and pull-up
Readily available in the store	More expensive than training pants in the long run

Training Pants: Pros and Cons	
Pros	Cons
Child feels wet after soiling	Difficult to clean up messes
Washable	Parents may have to do laundry more often, especially at the beginning
Saves money not having to buy disposable pull-ups	May not be as easy to find as disposables

"POTTY-FRIENDLY" CLOTHING

In order to successfully potty train, children will need clothing that they can easily take on and off. Jumpers, rompers, overalls, and one-piece pajamas are difficult for children to remove. If you haven't bought them already, consider buying sweat pants or stretch pants that have an elastic waist for your toddler to easily pull up and down. Being able to easily remove pants will minimize accidents that occur from not being able to make it to the potty quickly enough! Easily removable clothing will also give your child a sense of independence because they will be able to remove their own clothing without assistance. In addition, when you are potty training in earnest, try to avoid any articles of clothing with buttons, hooks, or snaps. These will also cause frustration for you and your child, and increase the potential for accidents.

Parent Point-of-View
"I suggest giving up all those cute overalls when you start potty training. I didn't and it was a disaster! The first time my son wanted to use the potty to pee, it was too late by the time I got all the snaps undone. Even after that I persisted, but finally gave up. Potty training is a learning process for everyone."

PLASTIC BED SHEETS

Believe it or not, some parents choose to get rid of diapers altogether once potty training has begun and just deal with accidents as they happen. Using plastic or waterproof bed sheets and mattress pads will protect the child's mattress, and help to contain nighttime accidents. It is important to note, however, that some children do not like the different feeling of plastic bed sheets. They may refuse to sleep in their bed if plastic bedding of any kind is used. If this is the case with your child, try placing the plastic item <u>underneath</u> the fitted sheet and mattress cover. It might be more comfortable for your little one (even though you will have to wash both the mattress cover and fitted bottom sheet if an accident occurs).

POTTY TRAINING DOLLS

There are a number of dolls and toys available to help parents teach their children about the physical process of potty training. These dolls usually come with a diaper and refillable bottle or cup that the doll "drinks" from. The doll then wets their diaper and needs to have it changed. These dolls can be fun for children and can help them make the link between drinking, peeing, and needing to have a diaper changed, though they are by no means necessary for teaching a child the process.

A Special Potty Training Companion

Children can also "teach" a familiar or favorite doll or stuffed animal to use the potty—even if the animal or doll is not specifically made for potty training purposes. Some children will enjoy having a familiar companion "learn" along with them. In addition, many parents find that the use of a favorite doll can speed up the training process if a child is particularly attached to a given toy. As you are training your child to use the potty, your child is training their doll to use the potty. This is a clever and powerful way to get young children engaged in the potty training process—especially those who love to mimic and imitate adults.

From *Sophie's Magic Underwear*,
Illustration by Valerie Bouthyette

There are many popular potty training dolls available for purchase at both traditional and online retailers. Browse around your local "big box" stores and also in children's toy stores.

> **Parent Point-of-View**
> "We got a potty DVD that my son loved. He watched it over and over and over again with his favorite stuffed bear and had the bear mimic the children in the video. It was amazing how much it inspired and interested him. Find something your child loves and stick with it!"

CHILDREN'S BOOKS ABOUT THE POTTY

As we mentioned before, children's books are available to help little ones learn about potty training. Many of these books contain familiar characters that make the child more interested in the story and overall process. Children's literature is also a reassuring and non-scary way for parents to present the idea of potty training to their child. Allowing the child to choose a book that they really like can help them to "own" the process, and make them more eager to begin potty training.

We recommend that you read any potty training children's book yourself before reading it to your child. Books that are written specifically for potty training are usually the most helpful. A new potty training children's book that emphasizes the <u>empowering</u> aspect of potty training is *Sophie's Magic Underwear*. This adorable book tells the story of young Sophie and how she successfully makes the transition to being a "big girl".

From *Sophie's Magic Underwear*,
Illustration by Valerie Bouthyette

For more information about *Sophie's Magic Underwear*, see the last page of this book.

POTTY CHARTS

Some children find rewards extremely motivating. Potty charts that allow children to earn stickers or checkmarks for each success are very popular with many parents and caregivers. These charts are usually hung at the child's eye level and near to where the "action" takes place (the bathroom wall, for example). The idea behind potty charts is that children are excited to get a sticker or check mark in *every* box, thus completing or filling out the whole chart. For some children, filling up the chart will be reward enough, whereas other children will need an additional motivational reward such as a "prize" for filling up the chart.

Potty charts do not need to be expensive, and can be easily made at home using a piece of colored paper, colorful markers, and inexpensive stickers. Exactly how you make the chart is limited only by your imagination and your immediate needs. The chart should reflect that potty training is a series of small victories and accomplishments. It should also be used as a tool for praising and reinforcing your child. If you decide to add a "prize" for meeting certain chart milestones (such as staying dry for a whole week), you can decide together with your child about the specific prize.

> ### Parent Point-of-View
> "Just three words of caution when it comes to potty training and using a reward system: Consistency, consistency, consistency! It is so important to remain one hundred percent consistent when you start a potty chart or motivational reward program. If you don't, you can inadvertently reinforce behavior you don't want, and risk confusing or frustrating your child."

MOTIVATIONAL REWARDS

Some children, particularly those that are not very excited about the prospect of potty training, may need more tangible rewards for potty training. Checkmarks or stickers on a chart may not be motivating enough for some youngsters. Remember that motivational rewards can be as simple as singing a special potty song after your child successfully uses the potty. Or, the reward may need to be something that the child specifically likes—such as a rubber stamp on the hand or their favorite small treat.

The Importance of Consistency

If parents use motivational rewards, they need to be consistent about giving a reward when it is promised. This will prevent the child from being disappointed and perhaps losing interest in the potty altogether. If a parent says that a reward is coming after a certain accomplishment and then the reward never materializes, the connection is broken between the accomplishment and the reward. If the child establishes a record of successes on the potty, parents may need to "change it up" and establish new goals that will merit rewards—such as rewarding the child each day instead of after each use of the potty.

Parent Point-of-View

"Don't start out with a giant reward. We made the mistake of offering our son a Thomas Train every time he earned six stickers for using the potty. The trains cost between $15 and $20 each, and we were buying two a week! It was too late to turn back once we started. The good news was that we were ALL motivated to complete potty training but it cost us a fortune in Thomas Trains. Our pride took a big hit too, when we had to explain to friends and family why we suddenly had a huge Thomas set and it wasn't even the holidays."

Great Ideas for Rewards

- Silly behavior from the parent such as a potty dance or song
- Stickers
- Coloring pages with favorite characters
- Extra television or computer time
- Small, inexpensive play figures or toys
- A Lego set or similar toy given one piece at a time
- A special trip to a museum or show
- M&Ms or a similar small treat given one at a time

- Special one-on-one time with a parent doing a favorite activity
- Calling family members with positive potty updates
- Family pajama party in the living room
- Baking a favorite recipe together
- Having a "potty party" with your child's favorite dolls
- Books or DVDs
- Taking a bus or train ride to somewhere special

Using Rewards: Pros and Cons	
Pros	Cons
Keeps child interested	Child can rely too heavily on external rewards instead of internal self-esteem
Reinforces positive behavior	If not consistent, you run the risk of reinforcing negative behavior
Gives everyone a structure for praise and tracking progress	You must be consistent to keep your child motivated

Parent Point-of-View
"One thing that worked great for us was upping the challenge for our son. Once he reached certain milestones consistently over a period of time, we went from earning a reward every day to earning a reward every three days, then every five days, etc., until his goals were met. We kept this up until we didn't need any reward at all. But every once in a while, I would reward him out of the blue and that was the most motivating of all."

EMERGENCY/TRAVEL KITS

Children who are in the process of potty training may have difficulty using the potty outside of their own home, and may need to temporarily use diapers or pull-ups while traveling. Parents should introduce their toddlers to toilet toppers, even if they use a potty chair, in case they are unable to bring the chair with them or if the child needs to use the toilet while on an outing. Parents should also carry a supply of diapers or pull-ups with them in case the child needs to use the toilet but is fearful or unwilling to do so. Accordingly, parents will also need diaper changing supplies such as wipes and ointment if the child will be using diapers at any point during travel. Parents should also carry a full change of clothing and plastic bags for wet clothing, as accidents will most certainly occur during travel. Taking the time to think through what you need in an emergency or travel kit will save you many headaches down the road.

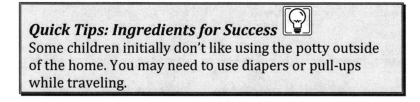

Quick Tips: Ingredients for Success
Some children initially don't like using the potty outside of the home. You may need to use diapers or pull-ups while traveling.

TODDLER WIPES

Pre-moistened wipes can be very helpful for wiping toddlers and for helping them to learn to wipe themselves. Toddlers and preschoolers have difficulty using toilet paper, particularly after a bowel movement. Pre-moistened wipes are much easier for little hands to use, and the single sheets mean they will be less likely to take too many and potentially clog the toilet. While many of these wipes come in colorful packages marketed specifically for use by children, more inexpensive, "adult" wipes that are sold in the toilet paper aisle can also be used and are safe for toddlers over the age of two.

Parents may elect to have the child use several squares of toilet paper first and then finish the job with a pre-moistened wipe, but it is more sanitary to do the opposite. First, wipe the child with the pre-moistened wipe, then have the child wipe with toilet paper to minimize the mess that may be left on little hands. Teach your child to wipe from front to back as this will help to prevent urinary tract infections, especially in little girls.

Parent Point-of-View
"We made a chart with pictures and words describing exactly the procedure we wanted our daughter to use in the bathroom. It was very simple. Every time she used the potty I went over the steps with her, including how much toilet paper to use and how to wipe front to back. It worked great in helping her learn the process and read some new words as well!"

HAND HYGIENE SUPPLIES AND TIPS

Toddler hygiene supplies such as hand sanitizer and hand soap come in large, colorful bottles with easy-to-use spouts. These items can help toddlers remember to wash their hands after using the potty, and are also fun for children to use! Just like anything else with young children, parents should monitor the use of these hand washing products since they can be incredibly fun to squirt and potentially generate a large mess. *Children should be encouraged to wash their hands after every use of the potty, even if they have only urinated.* Now is the time to establish good hygiene habits with your child. In addition, remember to model the same behavior that you want your child to display. When they see you washing your hands after using the bathroom, it reinforces the importance of consistent bathroom hygiene.

DIAPER LINERS

There are liners available to help children to feel wet while still wearing a disposable diaper. These are designed to go inside the diaper and change temperature when the child urinates—giving them a cold feeling immediately after urinating. Some disposable pull-ups already have these "feel wet" liners inside of them, and are marketed for this same purpose. These liners are made for parents who prefer to keep their child in a regular, disposable diaper while potty training. Of course, this product is completely optional, but many parents do find these liners to be helpful.

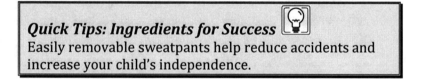

Quick Tips: Ingredients for Success
Easily removable sweatpants help reduce accidents and increase your child's independence.

POTTY TARGETS

Parents that want to teach their little boys to stand while urinating have many options for items that can be added to the toilet as "targets". These may include bull's eyes, Cheerios, or other small shapes that the child needs to "aim" at. While these can be fun for little boys, parents should be prepared to clean up the mess that will inevitably be made while teaching young boys—especially toddlers—how to urinate while standing up!

SUPPLIES CHECKLIST

Remember that the only required items for potty training are a willing child, a patient parent, and a toilet of some kind! A potty chair or toilet topper is almost a necessity, but parents that are patient and determined can do without them.

Turn to the next page to review our Potty Training Supplies Checklist. Take this handy list with you to the store when you are buying your potty training supplies. Simply circle the items you have chosen, and cross them off once you have put them in your shopping cart.

Potty Training Supplies Checklist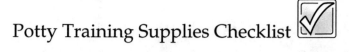

Necessary Items	Purchase Yes/No?	How Many?
Potty Chair		
Toilet Topper		
Training Pants		
Pull-ups		
Extra underwear and pants		
Footstool		
Travel or Emergency Kit		
• Diapers or pull-ups		
• Toilet topper		
• Wipes		
• Ointment		
• Full changes of clothing		
• Plastic bags		
Optional Items	Purchase Yes/No?	How Many?
Plastic Bed Sheets or Waterproof Pads		
Potty Training Doll		
Potty Training Children's Books		
Potty Chart		
Motivational Rewards (stickers, toys, candy)		
Diaper Liners		
Targets for the Toilet		
Pre-moistened Disposable Wipes		
Toddler Hygiene Supplies (soap, hand sanitizer)		

Go to www.lessonladder.com for a downloadable version of this checklist.

5

Pre-Potty Training
with Your Child

You may be curious about the phrase "pre-potty training." What does it actually mean? *Pre-potty training consists of all the things you do to lay the groundwork for actual potty training.* Instead of jumping headfirst into potty training, we recommend that you first <u>introduce</u> the concept to your child. Explain to them what it will involve, and excite them about taking this next step towards becoming a big girl or big boy. It's sort of like an advertisement for a new movie or television show that will be released within the next week or two. You want to get your child excited and ready for this upcoming big event!

Pre-potty training also starts with some detective work on your part as you begin looking for your child's unique patterns. It is essentially about pre-teaching your child so that once the training begins, everyone is on the same page. As we discussed in earlier chapters, parents are integral to the potty training process and should try to maintain a positive and encouraging tone throughout. The following "pre-potty" steps will ensure your child's success and provide them with a solid foundation for learning this important life skill!

PRE-POTTY STEP 1: LOOK FOR CLUES AND PATTERNS

Parents should keep an eye out for signals that the child is about to pee or poop. (For example: a child holding their crotch, or hiding in a corner to poop.) Once you begin potty training in earnest, these signals will be useful for determining when it is the right time to take your child to the potty. Each child, even children in the same family, show different signals for when they are about to poop or pee, so it is important that parents watch for different signals in each individual child.

A Little More about Pee and Poop Patterns

Like adults, children have timing patterns for when they will pee and poop. This may be first thing in the morning, before or after meals, or at certain other times of the day. Try to determine your child's unique elimination pattern for both peeing and pooping to know when you should take them to the potty. Taking your child to the potty when you know they are about to poop or pee is a great way to begin potty training, and helps your child begin to recognize their own bodily signals.

Toddlers usually need to pee between 30 and 90 minutes after drinking liquids. This, of course, can vary from child to child. Since older children have larger bladders, they do not need to pee as frequently as younger children. Poop patterns are different for every child. Some children poop once a day or once every other day and this is normal for them, while others may poop three or more times a day and also be considered normal. The average toddler poops twice a day, but this varies widely. You are probably already aware of your child's poop patterns as they require immediate diaper changes. You may need to do a bit more investigating to determine your child's pee patterns.

Common Signs and Signals

Signs that your child may need to pee include a changing facial expression, standing motionless, shifting from foot to foot, or holding their private parts. Signs your child is pooping may include grunting, straining, squatting, hiding, a reddened face, or changing facial expression. Children may look relieved or return to playing when they are done with peeing or pooping. Some children may remove their own diapers when they are finished peeing or pooping. As we said earlier, this indicates their discomfort in the soiled diaper, and is a great indication that they may be ready to begin potty training.

Heads Up!

As you continue introducing the concept of potty training to your child, it is helpful to encourage them to tell you when they have soiled their diaper. With further encouragement, your child may even begin to tell you *before* they pee or poop, which will give you the opportunity to get them to the potty beforehand. If they can recognize the need to go before they wet their diaper, they won't have to experience the discomfort of a soiled diaper. Working with your child to get them to tell you <u>before</u> they soil their diaper encourages them to become more aware of what their own body is telling them. The ability to recognize the need to pee or poop before it happens is a major milestone for a young toddler!

PRE-POTTY STEP 2: INTRODUCE YOUR CHILD TO THE POTTY

Before you begin the actual potty training process, you will want to expose your child to their new potty chair and show them the basics about how to use it. Children usually get very excited about using something new that was purchased especially for them! Introducing your child to their new potty in a non-threatening way is an important early step in the potty training process.

Location, Location

After you and your child decide on a potty, decide together where to place it. You may choose to put the potty chair in the bathroom so that your child can be near the adult toilet, or you can choose to put it somewhere closer to where your child spends most of their day. Parents often start out by placing the potty in the kitchen, family room, or playroom for this very reason. This makes the potty easier to reach when your child indicates the need to pee or poop. It can always be moved into the bathroom after the child has mastered their own bodily signals, and can get themselves to the potty before an accident. Giving your little one some initial input on where to place the potty will help to foster their independence and get them excited about the process.

Take a Seat!

After you have chosen the location for the potty chair, allow your child to practice sitting on their new potty while fully clothed. This allows them to get used to sitting down on the potty in a non-threatening way. You can also have your child sit clothed on the potty while you are using the bathroom yourself. This will give them a chance to become accustomed to sitting on the potty, and also to learn about using the potty as you explain what *you* are doing. This reinforces the idea that they can learn to do something that their parents do—a real sign of becoming a bigger kid!

Quick Tip: Getting Started
Early and enthusiastic exposure to the potty will help your child get excited about their upcoming adventure.

Reading Material

As we mentioned in earlier chapters, many parents choose to read potty training books with their children as a way of introducing them to the process. These stories usually depict a toddler going through the potty training process, and often show the character experiencing occasional accidents and setbacks before they finally become successful. These books are a great way to set a positive tone, and reinforce that potty training is all about learning and not giving up. Potty books can also be used as 'reading' material for your child while they are sitting on the potty waiting to poop or pee, or they can be used as bedtime stories to get your child excited about the process. Seeing photos and illustrations of other children on the potty (and their successes) can be very motivating!

> ### Parent Point-of-View
> "It's good to remember that potty training is like every other milestone that you and your child will go through together. There will be mistakes and accidents, successes and achievements. It's all part of life and the human experience. Embrace it all—there is joy in everything your child does—even if it's peeing in his pants! It is our job as parents to be there for our children and that's what matters most."

Pre-Potty Summary of Steps 1 and 2

- Choose a potty chair or allow your child to choose their own potty chair from the store.
- Decide together where you will place the potty chair, either in the bathroom or in the place where you child spends most of their time.
- Have your child begin practicing sitting on the potty while fully clothed.

- Consider bringing your child into the bathroom with you when you need to go, and talk about what you are doing.
- Read potty books to your child as they sit on the potty.

PRE-POTTY STEP 3: USE CONSISTENT LANGUAGE WITH YOUR CHILD

As the parent, it is important for you to decide which terminology you want to use when teaching your child to potty train. You have probably been talking to your child about potty terms ever since you have been changing their diaper. Of course, you can continue to use whatever terms you and your family prefer, understanding that daycare providers, preschools, and other caregivers may use different terms. Ask your child's other caregivers how they usually refer to potty terms so that your child doesn't become confused. "Poop" and "pee" might be more politely termed "BM" and "urine" in other settings—especially at school. You will also want to show your child what you mean by "wiping," "washing your hands" and even "going to the potty." They may not be familiar with these terms unless you have been using them during diaper changes.

Think also about the terms you will use for anatomy. You have probably already come up with your preferred terms for the "private parts," and these will become your child's favorite topics of conversation for months to come as potty training progresses! Many parents and child development experts recommend the use of the correct anatomical terms with children, such as "penis" and "vagina" so that children become comfortable using these words from the get go. Using nicknames for these body parts (such as "your pee-pee" or "your potty") is also fine as long as it is not confusing for your child, and as long as your child eventually learns the correct terminology.

We have included an interesting little table on some common terms for different body parts and bodily functions related to potty training. Which terms are you most comfortable with? Which do you plan to use with your child?

Common Potty Vocabulary

Medical Term	Common Term
Bowel Movement	Poop, poo-poo, BM, turd
Urination	Pee, urine, pee-pee, wee-wee, wee, tinkle
Flatulence	Fart, toot, stinky, fluff, wind
Buttocks	Butt, bottom, tush, tushie, rear, rear end, bum
Vagina (or vulva)	Pee-pee, privates, potty, 'gina
Penis	Pee-pee, wee-wee, wiener, privates

Sample Language for Two Year Olds

In addition to terminology, it's also important to think about the language you will use to actually get your child to the potty. Two year old children need more direction and simpler language than older children. Using simple, clear statements such as, "Now we're going to sit on the potty!", or "It's time to go sit on the potty!" work better for younger potty trainers than being given too much language and potentially confusing them.

Sample Language for Three Year Olds

Most three year old children are able to make choices, and will appreciate being able to make a decision or choice rather than being given constant adult direction. Giving your child choices will also help to foster independence. Asking questions such as, "Would you like to color or go for a walk after you use the potty?" or "Would you like a sticker or a stamp on your hand after you go to the potty?" still gives your child direction, but allows them some input into the process.

PRE-POTTY STEP 4:
MOTIVATE YOUR CHILD

When it comes to successful potty training, don't underestimate the importance of your child's motivation. Different children are motivated in different ways, and you should consider the approaches that will be most exciting to your child. If your child wants to be a "big kid," then talk about using the potty in a way that will make them feel older, such as: "Now that you are getting to be such a big boy/girl, we're going to learn to use the potty." If your child has no interest in being "big," consider motivating them by making them feel special. Many children find it incredibly motivating to have their own "special potty." You know your own child best, and you should talk about potty training in whatever way will be most exciting and motivating for them.

Motivating Different Personality Types

When thinking about motivation, you should also consider your child's unique temperament and personality. Goal-oriented children, for example, tend to be more motivated when parents give them something to work towards. Reward charts might therefore work very well for a goal-oriented child. Receiving a big prize for reaching the end of their potty chart is another ideal motivator for these personality types. After talking with your child, decide what the goal will be, and how you will accomplish it together.

Outgoing children are often motivated by being the center of attention. These children may be more motivated by a "party" model of potty training. (In other words, the bulk of potty training is performed during a "potty party weekend.") According to many parent reports, extroverted children also enjoy being rewarded and praised for each success—such as receiving a "mommy potty dance" or sticker for each successful behavior during the potty training process.

Children that are more shy or introverted will probably not want to be made the center of attention, and may not respond well to the "potty party" model. Keeping track of successes on a reward chart and giving a sticker or stamp on their hand after each successful behavior will probably be more motivating for these children. In other words, simple acknowledgement is preferred to celebration. While children with a shy personality type may not want a "show" after each success, they should still get plenty of positive motivation and encouragement from their parent or caregiver.

PRE-POTTY STEP 5: MODEL/DEMONSTRATE FOR YOUR CHILD

If your child has ever come in the bathroom with you while you are using the toilet, it is likely that she was watching, wondering, and learning what you were doing without you even realizing it! When you begin to introduce the concept of potty training, you will want to break down the exact steps for your child. It is helpful to slow down and explain exactly what you are doing while using the bathroom. This begins with telling your child how you pull down your pants before you start so that you won't get wet. You can then demonstrate how you sit down on the toilet with your feet on the floor, show them how the pee and poop goes into the toilet, and demonstrate how much toilet paper to use. Finally, you can then show them how you pull your pants back up when you are done, and wash your hands with soap and water.

Some children will want to mimic your every move when you first begin modeling appropriate potty behavior. Be sure to encourage any small amount of interest that you get from your child, especially in the beginning. Also, allow your child to wash their hands with you after using the potty since this is an important healthy behavior for them to learn. Have your child sing a song while washing hands so that they know about how long to wash. *The ABC Song, Row, Row, Row Your Boat,* and *Twinkle, Twinkle Little Star* are all about the right length of time for proper hand washing.

On the next page, we have included a quick and handy summary of the modeling points discussed above.

Parent Point-of-View

"Every mom knows that when she goes to the bathroom, it is somehow a signal to the entire family to barge in and ask questions. So, I was finally glad to have a valid reason to let my daughter in the bathroom! Not only did I use the opportunity to talk about using the toilet, I also took the opportunity to tell her that when she's a mommy she can explain the process to her children, too. However, I left out the part about how as a mommy she will never go to bathroom in peace again!"

Modeling for Your Child Summary

- When you need to go to the bathroom, take your child in with you.
- Have your child sit on or stand in front of their potty chair while you are using the bathroom.
- Tell them each step of the process as you do it ("Now I'm pulling down my pants so that my pee will go into the toilet. Now I sit down on the potty, etc.")
- Talk to your child about how the pee and poop goes straight into the toilet instead of into a diaper.
- Show your child how you choose the amount of toilet paper to use, and how it is different for pee and poop.
- After using the potty or going in the bathroom, have your child wash their hands with you while you sing a song to ensure you wash for at least 30 seconds with soap and water.

6

Potty Training:
The Nuts and Bolts!

CONGRATULATIONS! Now that you have determined that your child is ready to begin potty training, purchased all of the necessary supplies, and decided how you'll be rewarding each success, you are ready to begin the training process in earnest! Before we begin, however, let's briefly talk about you. What do <u>you</u> need to make potty training manageable?

YOUR PATIENCE PLAN

Before you throw yourself into the potty training process, recall our discussions about the importance of patience and positive energy. There will certainly be days when your child and the potty training process test your patience. What will you do if your child has multiple accidents in a day, or poops on the floor in protest? Before you officially begin your child's training process, take some time to develop a "patience plan" for yourself. Choose some specific actions that you can take to help yourself regroup when the going gets tough. Maybe it's a quick cup of tea and a few deep breaths in a separate room. Or perhaps it's some quick yoga poses or stretches. You could also ask a good mom or dad friend to be your on-call "potty buddy" so that you can call or text them for some quick support if you are having a tough day. It is totally normal for parents to have "ups and downs" during the potty training process. Just give yourself some time and space <u>now</u> to think about how you will cope during those difficult times.

Also, before you begin potty training, consider what language and strategies you will use with your child during those tough moments. If your child pees on the floor in protest, for example, it is best to remain neutral and not show your disappointment or exasperation. Children respond to big reactions, and you want to save your big reactions for their positive potty behaviors, not negative ones. Even though you may want to scream, you should simply and calmly say "pee and poop always go in the potty" (or something along these lines), and clean up in a similarly neutral fashion. We will discuss accidents and setbacks in greater detail later on, but it's a good idea to be pro-active and think now about how you will handle difficult moments with your child—<u>before</u> you find yourself in the throes of potty training.

THE 13 KEY STEPS OF POTTY TRAINING

Although there are many different methods of potty training, this book presents an approach that is universally accepted by many child development experts and pediatricians.

From *Sophie's Magic Underwear*,
Illustration by Valerie Bouthyette

Step 1: Be Consistent and Focused

- Begin potty training at a non-crazy time for your family when you have time and energy to devote to the process. You and other caregivers will need to be very responsive to your child's toileting cues, so choose a month or two when this focus will be possible.
- Make sure that all parents and caregivers are "on the same page" and able to follow through with the potty training protocol that you establish.
- Approach the potty training process systematically, as we have outlined in this book. For example: don't have your child wear a diaper one day and then big kid underwear the next day if they are not truly ready for that next step.
- Use a kitchen timer or an alarm on your phone to remind yourself to take your child to the potty on a set schedule—about once every hour.

Step 2: Consume Foods and Fluids That Will Help the Process

- Whole grains such as whole grain pastas, cereals, and breads are important for keeping the stool well formed. Eating fresh fruits and vegetables will also help to keep bowel movements soft and comfortable for your child.
- Starchy vegetables like potatoes and corn do not add bulk to the stool and should be avoided in the short-term if your child is having issues with bowel frequency.
- Encouraging extra fluids is important—both for keeping bowel movements soft, and for increasing urination. More fluids means that your child will need to pee more often—thus providing important opportunities for potty practice!
- If juice is your child's favorite beverage and s/he is drinking more of it during potty training, try to buy a

low sugar brand and remember to brush their teeth frequently.

> **Quick Tip: Increase Fluids and Motivation**
> *Encourage your child to drink from their own special water bottle that is especially made for "big boys and girls" who are learning how to use the potty!*

Step 3: Take Your Child to the Potty Often

- When you first begin potty training, getting your child to the potty chair in time is especially important so that they will experience success. Having early successes will keep both of you motivated.
- Remember that you will need to watch for your child's bodily signals of impending urination and bowel movements—especially because they are just learning how to recognize the signals themselves.
- Take your child to the potty about once every hour, whether or not they show the signals of needing to go. If you have increased your child's fluid intake, they will need to urinate every one to two hours at the very least.
- When you are first starting, consider letting your child wear minimal or no clothing when you are at home. Fussing with removal of clothes may impede your child's early successes.
- If your child does go without clothes in the beginning, you may have a few messes to clean up off the floor. However, these early accidents can be invaluable learning lessons for your child. They help them to connect their body's signals with the pee or poop that comes out.

From *Sophie's Magic Underwear,*
Illustration by Valerie Bouthyette

Step 4: Use a Potty Doll, Stuffed Animal, and Children's Potty Book

- Consider using a potty doll or your child's favorite stuffed animal to "show" them how to use the potty, especially if your child shows any fear at all. Seeing how dolly uses the potty and has fun sitting on it can help your child to feel safe in using the potty, too.
- Use a children's potty book to help your child understand the potty training process. Visit the LessonLadder.com website to purchase a copy of

Sophie's Magic Underwear, a brand new, beautifully illustrated children's book all about potty training.

Step 5: Praise and Encourage Your Child Often

- Praise every small action that your child takes at the beginning, whether it is pulling down their own pants, sitting on the potty by themselves, or actually going pee or poop on the potty. Every action is a victory, especially at the beginning.
- Many parents also praise their child for keeping "dry pants." Check their training pants or pull-up every half hour and give them praise for staying dry!
- Even after some potty success, continue the practice of praising your child for doing what you have taught them to do. It will keep them motivated and encouraged to continue using the potty.
- Remember to make your praise as specific as possible, so that your child knows exactly what they did right. ("Great job wiping, Billy!") You can also praise them for their effort and hard work, and not just what they produced on the potty.

Step 6: Give Wiping and Toilet Paper Lessons

- From the very beginning, teach your child proper wiping techniques in order to maintain good health and reduce the chance of urinary tract or bladder infections.
- Wiping from front to back is the correct way to wipe for both boys and girls, but is especially important for girls.
- Wiping is difficult for little ones as their arms don't yet reach to their behinds very well, and their hands don't yet have the fine motor coordination that is necessary for proper wiping.
- It is usually best if mom or dad wipes the child first, and then lets the child "finish up" the wiping process. This will teach your child the proper mechanics for when they are later able to wipe themselves.
- Expect that you'll be helping your child with wiping after bowel movements for several years, possibly into school age depending on your child's coordination and fine motor skills.
- Teach your child about toilet paper early in the potty training process—especially how much to use for each action. (For example, have your child use three squares for pee and six squares for poop).
- If you decide to use flushable wipes instead, teach your child to only wipe with one or two flushable wipes. You can explain in your own terms how the toilet might

break if you use too many wipes or too much toilet paper.

From *Sophie's Magic Underwear*,
Illustration by Valerie Bouthyette

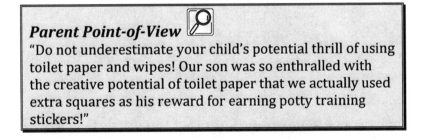

Parent Point-of-View

"Do not underestimate your child's potential thrill of using toilet paper and wipes! Our son was so enthralled with the creative potential of toilet paper that we actually used extra squares as his reward for earning potty training stickers!"

Step 7: Give Flushing Lessons

- Flushing can either be a fun or a terrifying experience for children, and it really depends on the child.
- Teach your enthusiastic flusher that they only need to flush once. They can flush again after making another pee or poop on the potty!
- If your child fears the flush, do not force the issue. It is OK if you flush for them. If they are only mildly afraid of the flush, you may want to encourage them to wave "bye bye" to the poop or pee as you perform the actual flush.

- If your child has a significant fear of flushing, you can wait until they have left the bathroom to flush. Children usually overcome this fear before they enter school.

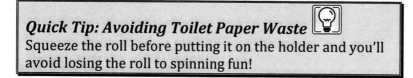

Quick Tip: Avoiding Toilet Paper Waste
Squeeze the roll before putting it on the holder and you'll avoid losing the roll to spinning fun!

Step 8: Give Hand Washing Lessons

- Proper hand washing prevents many illnesses and should be taught to children early in life.
- Everyone, including grownups, should be washing their hands after a trip to the potty. Just being in the bathroom leaves unwanted germs on the hands that need to be washed off with soap and water.
- Encourage your child to sing a short song while hand washing to ensure that they have washed long enough (such as The ABC Song). Alternatively, you and your child can make up your own hand washing song together.

From *Sophie's Magic Underwear,*
Illustration by Valerie Bouthyette

Step 9: Chart the Successes (and Misses)

- Early on in the potty training process, decide how and when you will chart your child's successes. Early efforts such as sitting on the potty or pulling down pants should earn a check mark, star, or sticker on your child's reward chart.

- Show your child how you give them a star or check mark after they have done something correctly, and be sure to show them plenty of enthusiasm when you do it!

- Keep your potty chart close to where the action is— somewhere near the potty chair.

- Keep track of your child's accidents as well so that you can be aware of any important patterns (such as always having an accident at a certain time of day), and their overall progress.

- After your child has mastered all the early skills of potty training (such as sitting on the potty chair), you may later transition to only charting large successes like actually pooping or peeing on the potty.

Step 10: Give Rewards

- You know your child best and understand what
  motivates them. Use this knowledge to choose the best
  ways to reward your child.
- Younger children may need immediate rewards, such
  as a small piece of candy, sticker, or hand stamp after
  each success.
- Rewards do not always have to be tangible. Some
  children are totally satisfied with a cheer or a "potty
  dance" from a beloved adult.
- Older children may be able to wait to earn enough stars
  or checks on their reward chart to "trade them in" for a
  bigger reward, such as a toy or a special treat.
- Decide when you will "change the rules" and only
  reward for a more advanced potty training behavior,
  such as actually peeing in the potty.

- Be sure to positively communicate the reward change to your child. You might tell them, "Now that you're so good at sitting on the potty, you're only going to get a sticker when you make pee. I know you can do it!"
- Stay enthusiastic and continue to provide plenty of praise, even as you change the goals.

Parent Point-of-View
"Think about how good you feel when someone praises your efforts or appreciates the hard work that you have done. Now think about how much more a child enjoys that kind of positive attention. Never be stingy when it comes to praising your child for accomplishments!"

Step 11: Switch to Training Pants or Pull-Ups

- When you start potty training, consider using washable, cloth training pants. These may seem old fashioned, but they are very effective for teaching potty training. Children who have worn disposable diapers their entire lives will definitely feel the wetness when they wear training pants and have an accident.
- Get some plastic pants for your child to wear over the training pants, especially for when you need to be out of the house or away from home for any length of time. Plastic pants will help keep messes to a minimum while still allowing your child to feel wet when they have peed or pooped.
- If you need to use pull-ups instead of training pants, choose the kind that will allow your child to actually feel when they are wet or soiled.
- Once your child has achieved some potty training success, take them out on a special shopping trip to buy real "big kid" underwear!
- Before your child goes on an outing in "big kid" underwear, make sure that they can stay dry at home in underwear for several hours at a time. Success builds upon success!

Step 12: Move from the Potty to the Toilet

- Unless you began there, moving from the potty chair to the big toilet is usually the last step in the potty training process.
- Making the move from potty chair to toilet may take several months, and should only be initiated after your child has experienced consistent success on the potty.
- The large opening in the adult toilet can be scary for many children. They may have a legitimate fear of falling in. Make sure that you use a toilet topper or seat adjuster to prevent any possibility of falling in.
- Young children should always have an adult nearby when they are using the adult toilet. An adult can monitor the situation and make sure that everyone stays safe, clean, and dry when using the "big" potty.

Step 13: Be Patient!

As we have said over and over, try to stay patient and calm. There will be accidents, setbacks, and even some regressions, but a positive and supportive approach is essential for your child's success. Think of yourself as your child's partner on a great adventure—their first of many. You are there to teach, encourage, praise, and support them as they work towards achieving this major goal.

From *Sophie's Magic Underwear*,
Illustration by Valerie Bouthyette

OTHER APPROACHES TO POTTY TRAINING

As we explained above, this book outlines a tried-and-true approach to toilet training that is endorsed by many parents and child development experts. Let's take a few minutes to review a few other popular potty training approaches that you might be hearing and thinking about.

Fast Track Training

The "boot camp" approach, also known as Potty Training in a Day, was a popular approach to potty training in the recent past. This method is not for all children, and parents have to be very committed, resilient, and firm for the method to work at all. This "fast track" approach can be overwhelming for many children, and may cause setbacks or the need for potty training to be abandoned altogether for a time.

What is Fast Track Training?

The method is fairly simple and consists of planning for a full day of potty training. You need a doll that wets, training pants, a potty chair, and lots of liquids that your child likes and will drink. With this method, parents give their children a lot of liquids—anything the child is willing to drink and as much of it as they will drink, which will cause the child to need to pee more so that they can practice using the potty. The reward for using the potty is more liquids—again, as much as the child will drink. If the child has an accident, they have to sit on the potty afterward to "learn" what they should have done so that they will get it right the next time. Children spend the day with a doll that wets itself and practice with the doll, giving it a bottle or cup of liquid, pulling down its underwear, and having it use the potty. The doll is used in between the child's own potty visits while they are themselves drinking fluids.

Parents have to be able to be very strict with this method, but cannot be punishing in any way. This method has rules that must be followed—fluids have to be consumed, and the child must use the potty when they need to pee or be placed on the potty after an accident without any exceptions. Parents that are successful with this method have plenty of patience and positivity. This method can be extremely frustrating, and parents that quickly lose their patience should not use this method, as negativity will thwart any progress.

Children that are successful with this method tend to be very cooperative in nature and must be able to follow instructions exactly. Younger toddlers are often not ready intellectually to follow directions, and older toddlers may be so independent that they will not follow directions. Parents need to catch the child at just the right developmental moment for this method to be successful, in addition to having a child with the right temperament.

> **Parent Point-of-View**
> "No matter what method you use to potty train, it is so important to be positive and supportive. Flexibility is the key as well. If your chosen method isn't working, be able to change course. It's healthy for everyone!"

Potty Training Party Weekend

The "potty party" method can be useful for older toddlers that love being the center of attention and are goal-oriented. You and your child choose a weekend for the "party", and that is the date that your child will no longer wear diapers. Parents will make a big deal about "the day," and talk about it for several weeks leading up to the date you have chosen.

How Does the Potty Party Method Work?

When the party day arrives, parents wait until after the child has peed in their diaper and then change them into "big kid" underwear or training pants. Parents make a big deal about the change, and the celebration often begins with clapping, singing, and celebrating, just like a birthday party or other special celebration. Children sometimes have a real party with guests, or may just have a party with their dolls and toys, and everyone celebrates that the child is now a "big kid."

Parents help their child by having them sit on the potty every 90 minutes for at least one minute. Accidents are treated as no big deal, and parents remind their children to use the potty the next time they feel like they are going to pee, helping them to understand their body's signals. Parents stay positive, and remind their child that they are now a "big kid" and don't need diapers anymore. They will now only use the potty when they need to pee.

This method can work very well for children that are able to set goals, or that show pride in accomplishments. Children that love being the center of attention may also be successful with this method. Children that are shy do not usually respond well to the "potty party" method and may become upset by having to be the star of the show. Parents also need to be patient and willing to deal with a number of accidents as the child learns about their bodily signals and when they need to pee.

> **Parent Point-of-View**
> "Just like in life, you have to follow your instincts and do what you feel is best for your child. It's hard sometimes, with pressure from friends, family, doctors, and even the media—but when you know what is best for your child and your family, you have to find the courage to follow your instincts."

Baby Track Method

The "baby track" method is gaining popularity with some parents, and is used in many cultures around the world. This method was also used in the early 20th century and has come back into fashion recently as parents seek to use fewer disposable diapers to protect the environment.

Many books have been written on the subject of the "baby track" method. The premise is that parents begin watching for their infant's signals that they are about to pee or poop, and hold them over a potty chair to go. Parents usually begin this method when the baby is about two months old, and will usually be successful within a few weeks of paying attention to the signals. When the child is able to sit up independently, they are taken to the potty and sat down on the potty chair. If the method works, the child learns to use the potty chair by the time that they can walk.

The advantages to this method are obvious—no diapers and no potty training at all. Children are already "potty trained" by the time they can walk. This method is appropriate for parents that are able to stay home with their child into the second year of life because an adult will need to get the child undressed when they signal they are about to need to use the potty. Most daycares are not able to support this method, so it is not very useful for parents that work outside the home.

No Pressure Potty Training

The final alternative method to potty training is one that more and more experts and pediatricians are beginning to recommend—no potty training at all. This method advises that the parents get a potty chair when the child shows an interest in what their parents are doing in the bathroom. The child then learns to use the potty themselves. Parents put no pressure on their child to use the potty or not to use the potty; the child simply begins going to the bathroom on the potty when they feel like it.

This method is great for children that have shown no interest in using the potty, and whose parents are able to allow them to stay in diapers for as long as is necessary. Most, if not all, children will "train themselves" by the time they go into kindergarten if not before, simply through natural maturation. This method respects the child's growing emotional and intellectual maturity, and allows them to learn on their own time and as a result of their own interest, not the interest of others. This method doesn't work for parents that send their child to a daycare where the child is expected to be out of diapers by two-and-a-half, or who need to get their child out of diapers for skin care or health care reasons.

7

Common Problems
and Obstacles

Potty training may go very smoothly for some families, but others find the process challenging for a variety of reasons. This chapter will briefly outline the most common problems and frustrations that parents experience during the potty training process. We hope that this section helps you prepare for any potty training "curveballs" that might come your way.

AN UNCOOPERATIVE OR RESISTANT CHILD

Occasionally, there are young children who do not want to participate in the potty training process at all. This can be frustrating for both the parent and child, and can lead to power struggles. If you have noticed that your child is not cooperating with your efforts to potty train, evaluate whether or not they are truly ready for potty training. You will need to determine their readiness based upon your parent-child bond, and your knowledge of their place on the readiness spectrum. Of course, we encourage you to use the Readiness Checklists included in Chapter 1: *Quick Summaries to Get You Started*, to help with this task.

If your child is older and is obviously ready for potty training, try to determine if there is something else standing in the way of their cooperation. If your child is already going through a major life change, such as starting preschool or welcoming a new sibling into the family, it may be less stressful for both of you if you can wait to begin potty training. One major life change may be all your child can handle at one time, which is perfectly understandable. If you are unable to wait because of daycare restrictions, you may want to find an alternate daycare provider for a short period of time while you wait for the emotional turmoil to subside. Also consider increasing pre-potty training efforts, such as reading potty training books, watching potty videos, and playing with potty dolls. (See Chapter 5: *Pre-Potty Training with Your Child*, for more information.) Maybe even let your child put stickers on a potty chart rewarding you, the parent, for going to the potty!

Allowing your resistant child to take the lead with potty training will benefit both of you, and will help with power struggles. Children are, after all, in charge of their own bodies and can decide for themselves when and if they will use the potty. Forcing a child that is showing resistance to potty training may be setting up both of you for additional power struggles as time goes on. Rest assured that your child will indeed become potty trained, likely before entering school. Your support and encouragement with potty training will set up your relationship for future successes as your child enters school, and as other new challenges present themselves.

Of course, if your child exhibits ongoing defiant behavior that concerns you, like an excessive number of tantrums per day, do not hesitate to contact your pediatrician. There are supports available for young children (and their parents) who need help dealing with emotional and behavioral issues.

AN UNINTERESTED OR BARELY INTERESTED CHILD

There are children who show absolutely no interest in using the potty. Perhaps they are too young, or do not have a clear understanding of why they would ever need to use the potty—especially when they have you to change their diapers! Depending on why they are disinterested, children can sometimes be persuaded to begin the potty training process.

If your child is on the younger side, they may not be able to fully understand what is going on just yet. They may not be emotionally mature enough to understand the potty training process. If emotional immaturity is the case, the remedy is simply time. Give them a few more months, and then reintroduce the concept of potty training. Your child will become ready and interested if given enough additional time to mature.

If you have an older toddler who seems able to understand the concept of going poop and pee on the potty but is still uninterested, they may need some additional motivation to stop using diapers. This may mean changing them into training pants before you begin potty training so that they are able to feel what is going on when they poop or pee. You may find, however, that your child still doesn't care about soiling their pants. If you find that training pants don't help, you may need to change your motivational tactics.

> **Parent Point-of-View**
> "Know your child and adjust. Flexibility is the key to parenting and potty training, and admitting when you have taken the wrong path is essential. Don't be afraid to make a mistake, but don't be afraid to admit it and fix it either!"

Use Bigger Rewards

Encouraging older children (closer to 3 years old) who do not care about soiling themselves may mean using larger rewards. This may mean a big toy or large reward that you know your child really wants. Older children may respond to this approach, but you will need to set the goals high in order for it to work long term. This method usually works best with a reward chart, where your child earns a number of "stars" in order for the prize to be achieved. An example might be offering a new tricycle as the reward for your child going poop on the potty twenty times. This can be easily set up on a reward chart with twenty boxes that need check marks, and a photo of the new tricycle at the end. Older children often understand the concept of delayed gratification, and having them repeat the wanted action a number of times should help them to learn the behavior that you want them to achieve—using the potty to poop and pee. After they have been successful, you can make a celebration of their "earning" the reward, and encourage them to continue using the potty afterward. If you find they regress into old patterns after having their success, you may need to think of an additional large reward, but keep setting the bar higher each time. For example, perhaps they need to make 50 successful poops in the potty before the next large reward.

Uninterested children can usually become interested if they are old enough to know that you want them to do something specific. Additional time or bigger rewards will almost always get the uninterested child to eventually succeed in using the potty.

THE FEARFUL CHILD

Some children fear using the potty. These children may fear the unknown, or may have had a prior negative experience with the potty. If your child had a negative experience, time will usually heal their fears. They may need some additional time to get the courage to try again. Try to be supportive and encouraging as any negativity toward their fear will only cause the child to continue to be fearful. Using statements like, "We'll use the potty as soon as you're ready," will let your child know that you still want them to use the potty, but respect the fact that they are not yet ready to do so. Your support and some additional time is usually all that is needed to cure their fear of the potty.

ACCIDENTS AND OTHER SETBACKS

Even children that potty trained easily or that have been potty trained for some time can have setbacks. Young children will commonly have some regressions when new baby siblings come home, or when they are introduced to new situations like preschool or daycare. Accidents may happen anytime during early childhood and are an expected part of the potty training process. While setbacks are troubling for parents, rest assured that they are completely normal.

Accidents Do Happen

Accidents are common among both toddlers and preschoolers, and usually resolve on their own by the time the child enters first grade, around age six. Accidents can happen for any number of reasons, from fear of public restrooms to not wanting to interrupt play when nature calls. Potty accidents are a part of childhood, and should be expected by parents. Accidents are almost never a sign of a power struggle and are usually only a sign that the child is not quite physically or emotionally ready to use the potty all of the time.

You can help to prevent accidents by encouraging your child to use the potty regularly, especially when they are busy at play. Reminding your child to use the potty on a regular schedule will help to prevent some accidents, but understand that accidents can and will still happen—even with frequent reminders to go to the potty.

From *Sophie's Magic Underwear,*
Illustration by Valerie Bouthyette

The Importance of Remaining Neutral

When accidents happen, try to be very matter-of-fact and neutral. Do not threaten or shame your child. Cleaning up an accident may be frustrating for you and embarrassing for your little one (especially as they get older), but it is an expected part of the potty training process. You can simply and neutrally inform your child that you need to get them cleaned up. Accidents that happen after your child has been potty trained for more than one year are usually a sign that they are not listening to their bodily signals. Your child may need more frequent reminders to use the potty, and may need to be interrupted from play to use the potty before an accident happens. Do not threaten your child with diapers or discipline after an accident, even if they are old enough to "know better." Try to determine what may be causing the accidents, and intervene before they happen.

ONE STEP FORWARD, ONE STEP BACK?

Setbacks and regression are common, especially in the first year of potty training. Baby siblings tend to come along around the same time as young children begin potty training, and can be a major cause of regression in young potty trainees. Seeing a new baby getting much of the attention in the house can cause not only accidents, but may also cause your little one to ask to go back into diapers for a time. This is usually temporary and may cause more work for you as a parent, but it is often less of a headache to allow your child to return to diapers for a month or two (as opposed to constantly cleaning up accidents).

Here's the good news. Children that have been potty trained for a while will usually only use diapers again for a short time. It is common for them to begin using the potty again by choice—after deciding that diapers are no longer for them. Some children, however, may need a bit more encouragement. You may consider putting them in cloth diapers or training pants to hasten their return to the potty. Most children, especially those that have been successfully wearing underwear, will not want to experience the feeling of wet diapers or training pants.

HOLDING IT

Believe it or not, parenting experts used to recommend that children learn to "hold it" to train their bladders and bowels. This is now recognized as a poor practice and can lead to many different problems in children, including urinary tract infections. For example, some children choose to "hold it" instead of using a public restroom. Some children "hold it" so long that their bladder becomes distended, which can lead to problems with the ability to sense the urge to urinate.

Fear of Public Restrooms

If you have noticed that your child holds their urine for longer than about two hours, encourage them to use the potty. If you are out in public and your little one won't use the public restroom, consider bringing along some disposable pull-ups, or investing in a portable potty chair that you can carry in your car for emergency situations. Many children are willing to use a potty seat or toilet topper that rests on top of the toilet, while others will not go anywhere near a public toilet.

Many children fear public restrooms because of the sound or type of flushing mechanism; they can be loud and scary to young ears. Automatic flushers can be alarming for many children and may make them unwilling to use a toilet that does not manually flush. As there is usually no way to interfere with the automatic flushing mechanism, you may need to either find an alternative restroom, or use a pull-up in these situations. If your child fears even entering a public restroom, it may be best to keep a potty chair in the car that is only used in emergency situations. Each child is different and will have their own comfort level and preferences for how and where they will use the potty outside of the house.

Parent Point-of-View
"My fourth child was absolutely terrified of automatic toilets. When she was first potty training, we learned which stores had them, and which did not. Those stores without automatic flushers got much more of our business for several years! She finally outgrew the overwhelming fear of the automatic toilets, but still does not like to use them. My son, on the other hand, refused to use any restroom outside of our house for any reason until he was about five years old. We had to plan trips and outings around his potty schedule. On a trip to Disneyland when he was four, he asked to go back to diapers for the week rather than have to use a 'foreign' toilet."

Try to go with the flow of your toddler or preschooler. If they are terrified of public restrooms, give them time to overcome this fear. With time and maturity, most children usually do. In the meantime, carry plenty of supplies with you, including changes of clothing for your child in case they try to "hold it" and then have an accident. Try not to be harsh with them and understand that they will overcome their fears in time and with your support.

NIGHTTIME INCONTINENCE

Many young children are not able to stay dry through the night. Nighttime incontinence, which is the technical term for involuntary loss of bladder control, is common among young children and considered normal until about age nine. The ability to gain nighttime bladder control relates to a child's overall physical development, and some children develop this skill much later than others. This can be embarrassing for some youngsters, particularly as they get older (6 or 7 years old).

There are several brands of pull-ups that are made for nighttime incontinence, and your child can be assured that there is nothing wrong with needing to wear these at night so that they can stay dry. Bladder control will develop when your child's body is ready for it. If your child starts waking up with a dry diaper or overnight pull-up several times per week, this is a good sign that their ability to keep dry overnight is emerging. In addition, many parents have found a night-time potty alarm system to be helpful for older children who are deep sleepers and have a hard time waking up to pee in the middle of the night. These nighttime potty alarm systems can be researched and purchased online.

If you are concerned about your child's continued nighttime incontinence, please don't hesitate to consult with your family doctor or pediatrician. Of course, you should also revisit this issue at their annual checkup each year. There are now some medications available that children can take to minimize nighttime incontinence, and you should discuss this option with your doctor if this has become an increasing and ongoing concern.

Bedwetting

While nighttime incontinence is considered normal until age nine, those children that have been dry for years and suddenly begin bedwetting are most likely having other issues. Emotional turmoil is the most common cause of bedwetting among children, and bedwetting accidents can occur during times of family disruption such as a move or a divorce, or during times of major change such as beginning school or changing schools. If there has not been a major life change in your family, you may need to delve further into what is going on with your child. They may be having difficulties in school or with their personal relationships. If you are not able to find out what might be emotionally upsetting your child, consider the possibility of a urinary tract infection. This can be tested at the doctor's office with minimal invasiveness and can usually be easily treated.

Occasional bedwetting accidents may occur with some children for no apparent reason. If you are not able to determine a direct cause (such as too much water drinking before bed), and no infection is found, consider using pull-ups for a short time—just to contain accidents and allow your child to sleep. If bedwetting continues, be sure to check with your pediatrician or family doctor for other possible causes.

8

Special Situations

As you have probably figured out by now, life with young children is never boring! You and your family may encounter certain situations or circumstances that make successful potty training more challenging. This chapter will present a quick overview of some of the most common "special circumstances" experienced by families with young children. If you find yourself in need of advice for a special situation, your pediatrician or family doctor is a great resource for ideas and strategies. Since they talk to hundreds of patients each year, they have literally "seen it all". Your pediatrician's office will also be able to steer you towards other community resources that might be helpful, such as parent support groups, counselors, and parent education organizations.

DAYCARE POTTY TRAINING

As we explained earlier, daycare providers have great incentive to want your child potty trained. Some daycare centers find it difficult to juggle multiple toddlers at various stages of the toilet training process. Many child care centers or preschools even require that your child be potty trained before they can be enrolled. If your daycare does accept toddlers who are still in diapers, or if they offer potty training at the daycare itself, be sure to check that the methods they use for potty training agree with your own, and that your child will not be pressured to use the potty before they are ready.

Some children will begin potty training at daycare and refuse to use the potty at home. Children sometimes like the "special time" they get with you when you are changing their diapers. Try to be supportive and encouraging of your child and give them the extra time they need with you after a long day at daycare. This may mean you sitting in the bathroom with them while they are on the potty—at least for several months while the potty training process is ongoing.

Parent Point-of-View

"My youngest daughter did not start daycare until she was nearly two. They immediately began working on potty training with her even though she had shown no interest at home. My daughter couldn't be in the 'big kid' class and was not allowed to play on the 'big' playground until she was out of diapers, which was enough incentive for her to finish potty training without any pressure at home. Her potty training progressed much more quickly than it did with my other children thanks to the support of my daycare provider, and she was fully potty trained within several months."

BABY SITTERS AND OTHER HELPERS

You may need to make your method of potty training very clear to those that come into your house to help. Baby sitters, family members, and friends often have their own ideas about potty training which can make the process confusing for your little one. *Be sure that everyone involved in your child's life is on the same page before potty training begins.*

Your mother, mother-in-law, and grandmother may have very different ideas about how best to potty train your child. Potty training methods have changed significantly since you were a child, but they may not realize this! While you should certainly hear them out, be clear that you have decided to pursue potty training with your child using your own methods, and let them know that potty training needs to proceed in your house by your rules. While it can be difficult to confront family members on parenting issues, know that it will help to prevent confusion for your child (and stress for you)!

Baby sitters should be given clear instructions about how and when to encourage your child to use the potty. To ensure consistency, show them the methods you use, including any rewards that are usually given after successful use of the potty. Expect that there may be some accidents, but short term baby sitting in your own home usually does not cause any problems or setbacks during the potty training process as long as everyone is on the same page.

SEPARATED PARENTS, TWO HOMES

Some children share time with parents living in separate homes. Coordinating potty training can be difficult, especially if each parent has a different idea about how potty training should proceed. Before any potty training begins, you will need to sit down with your co-parent and decide what your methods for potty training will be. Children who are potty training need consistency, and it is vital that you both decide together how potty training will work for your child.

After you and your co-parent discuss the basics of potty training, it can be helpful to purchase identical supplies for both homes. This means purchasing two potty chairs, having similar reward charts, and the same kind of wipes in both locations. Having everything the same in both houses will help your child with consistency, and will prevent them from playing the two parents against each other. When the rules are the same in both locations, there is no, "but Dad lets me do it this way…" or "Mom says I can have this…" which will make for less-stressed parents and a more easily potty trained child.

ON THE ROAD AGAIN

Travel sometimes poses problems for children because it takes them out of their routine. Traveling can be a problem for both children and parents during the potty training process because it can be difficult to take your child to the potty on a consistent schedule. It may also be difficult for children who do not like using public restrooms. You can try bringing along your child's potty chair and attempt to get them to use it either in the restroom or in the car. You can also offer them a reward for using a toilet topper, or for using new "big" potties during the trip. These strategies do not always work, and some children may protest and insist on an alternative—usually a return to pull-ups or diapers.

If your child refuses to use the potty while they are traveling, don't despair. Allowing them to choose the solution (usually returning to diapers for a time) shows that you support them, and also gives them a feeling of some control. Do try to encourage your child to use the potty during the trip, but allow them to make their own choices about how and where they will use it. Knowing that you support what is best for them will only strengthen the potty training process when you return home.

SLEEPOVERS

Children usually don't begin having sleepovers until they are of school-age which makes potty training less of an issue. If your school-age child still uses night-time pull-ups, they can still go on sleepovers with some help from you. Your child probably already knows that most school-age children do not wear pull-ups to bed, though it is more common than either of you might think. Tell your child that they will need to wear a pull-up during the sleepover to prevent any unwanted accidents from occurring during the night. Your child should be able to put on their own pull-up and put it on well before bedtime. Teach your child how to properly dispose of the pull-up in the morning, or provide a Ziploc bag to bring along to the sleepover.

It will be helpful for you to talk to the parent hosting the sleepover and explain the situation. Tell the parent that your child still needs pull-ups at night, and that your child can take care of the pull-up independently. Allow your child or the parent to call you if there are any problems. Most parents are very understanding when it comes to nighttime incontinence, as it happens to most children from time to time.

A FULL HOUSE:
POTTY TRAINING MULTIPLES

Parents of multiples understand that each of their children is different and develops on their own timetable, even if they are identical. This is true for potty training, too. While multiples may potty train together and may even find it fun to do so, most develop in their own time and will potty train in their own individual way and on different schedules. Just as older and younger siblings do things in their own time and way, so do multiples.

Each of your multiples should be treated individually while potty training, though you can encourage them to try to potty train together. This will mean allowing each child to pick out their own potty chair and underwear. It may even mean using different methods of potty training for each child, depending on what methods work for each of them. Allow each child to progress on their own timeline, just as you would if they were a singleton. Potty training multiple children may mean more work for the parent, but just take your time and get the support you need. In addition, remember that it is important not to compare children or encourage competition.

CHILDREN WITH SPECIAL NEEDS

Children with special needs may need more time to fully master potty training. Depending upon the needs of the individual child, potty training should be encouraged and supported, but should not be forced. If you have a child with identified special needs, you should consult your pediatrician early on and ask for guidance about potty training. Also, if your child receives therapeutic services from an early intervention provider or the public school system, your case manager or main contact should be able to help you access the appropriate potty training resources.

Children that have physical disabilities may need additional assistance from you to be successful. Just as with any other child, you should learn the signals that your child is getting ready to urinate or have a bowel movement, and get them to the potty in time. This may mean that you need to physically get them to the potty chair and help them undress. Even with physical limitations, children can learn to recognize their own bodily signals and let you know when they need to go. Children with physical limitations may also need additional help with wiping. Again, the physical therapists and other service providers working with your family should be able to guide you through the toileting process as it relates to your child's special needs.

If your child takes any special medications, you should check with your doctor to find out if they might have a constipating effect. You may need to alter your child's diet to promote easier bowel movements. This will further promote their success in potty training.

POTTY MOUTH

Children who are potty training often become fascinated by the new words you are teaching them about the process. Children may speak inappropriately or in inappropriate places while they are learning the vocabulary of potty training. While you shouldn't scold your child for using their new words, you may want to redirect them into the restroom when they begin their "potty talk." Instead of saying, "We don't say those words," say something to the effect of, "We only use those words when we're using the potty."

Children of potty training age are already fascinated by their bodies and their abilities. Having words to name their private parts can be irresistible to young children, and they should be allowed to use their new words in appropriate places. Taking them into the bathroom to allow them to talk freely about their "penis" or "vagina" can help your child verbalize freely while teaching them that certain words are only appropriate for the bathroom.

> ***Parent Point-of-View***
> "Try not to laugh when your child uses potty mouth, and try not to get upset either. They love to evoke an extreme reaction in you and once they see they can, they will keep trying to do it!"

URINARY TRACT INFECTIONS

Urinary tract infections, or UTIs, are a potentially serious infection of the tube that leads from the opening of the urethra to the bladder. If the infection persists, it can lead to a kidney infection and further problems.

Children usually complain of pain during urination when they have a UTI. They may also complain of abdominal pain ("tummy aches") or pain in their private parts when they are not urinating. They may also feel like they need to urinate and are not able to go. The test for a UTI is simple and can be performed in your pediatrician's or family doctor's office and merely consists of your child urinating into a special bowl in the toilet. If your child is unwilling or unable to urinate, a catheter can be inserted to collect some urine for testing. Treatment for a UTI usually consists of oral antibiotics and an increased intake of fluids.

You can help your child prevent UTIs by encouraging adequate fluid intake and hand washing after every visit to the bathroom, whether there was success on the potty or not. Little hands are usually not very clean, and should be washed often, especially during the potty training process. Frequent hand washing should include plenty of soap and water, and parents and caregivers should wash their hands after each time in the bathroom as well.

POOP PLAY

Though it seems disgusting to adults, playing with poop is not usually offensive at all to young children. If you catch your child playing with their poop, it is important not to appear disgusted, as you may hamper further efforts in potty training. Children should be taught that poop has germs and is waste that our body doesn't need, so we don't want to play with it. It needs to be flushed away each and every time. Your child can sense your feelings of disgust and may feel shame, which could cause a delay in successful potty training or resistance to the potty training process.

You can decrease the chances of poop play by showing your child early on what you do with the poop in their diaper. Take your child into the bathroom, and let them watch as you flush the poop down the toilet. You can let them wave "bye-bye" to the poop and explain that we flush it away because we don't need it any more. Be sure to thoroughly wash your hands and theirs after you say goodbye to the poop, and explain that since poop has germs, we need to clean our hands with soap every time after we flush. This will help your child get the message that poop is not clean without overtly saying that you find it disgusting!

OH, UNWANTED ADVICE!

You've probably received plenty of unwanted advice since bringing your baby into the world, and the beginning of potty training seems like an open invitation for well meaning people to provide you with even more. You can listen to the advice and take what you want from it. You may receive a helpful tip or two from friends that have been through potty training recently. Or, you may wholeheartedly disagree with everything they say. Let people know that you are trying your own methods, but appreciate that they care enough about you and your child to give you advice.

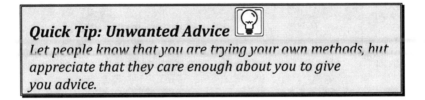

Quick Tip: Unwanted Advice
Let people know that you are trying your own methods, but appreciate that they care enough about you to give you advice.

CONSTIPATION

Constipation can happen for a number of reasons at any time during the toddler and preschool years. Some children may be anxious about pooping on the potty, or having to poop at school or places other than home, and will instead hold it in which causes constipation. Others do not get enough fiber or fluids in their diet and have hard stool that is difficult to pass. Regardless of the cause of constipation, it needs to be addressed quickly before other problems develop. Encouraging a diet that is rich in whole grains, fruits, vegetables, and plenty of water will prevent most cases of diet-induced constipation. This dietary approach is good for most children, whether they are potty training or not.

Children that fear pooping in the toilet need to be reminded about what poop is (bodily waste), and be assured that it is not part of their body that they are flushing away. You may need to allow your child to wave goodbye to the poop before flushing, or you may need to allow them to poop in a diaper until the fear subsides. Gentle encouragement and support are usually all that is required to alleviate fear of pooping on the potty. This fear usually passes with time, exposure, and maturity.

Encopresis is the medical term for long-term constipation. It is usually loose stool or diarrhea that passes around a hard mass of stool that has formed in the bowels. Children are usually not able to feel this stool passing, and it is often found as an "accident" in their pants. Children with encopresis may also wet themselves as the sphincter that holds the urinary tract closed may also open when stool is passed. This condition is serious and may need to be treated with an enema or other means as determined by your doctor. If you suspect that your child may have encopresis as evidenced by loose stool accidents several times a day in an otherwise well child, take them to your family doctor or pediatrician as soon as you can.

THE BEDTIME BATTLE

To help prevent nighttime accidents, you should always encourage your child to visit the potty before bed. Some children may quickly realize that they can put off bedtime by making frequent trips to the bathroom. Set firm limits with your child. While you certainly don't want to discourage them from using the potty if they need to, set limits on how many times you are willing to allow them to get up to use the potty after they have gone to bed. Children will test these limits, so it is important to be firm. If it is obvious that your child is trying to avoid bedtime, it is fine to tell them no more using the potty until morning. If they seem to truly need to use the bathroom multiple times before going to bed, try to determine what else might be going on.

TRICKY QUESTIONS

Children find the new terminology of potty training fascinating, and may ask you some "personal" or seemingly inappropriate questions—maybe even at inappropriate times. (For example: "Mommy, why do you and Daddy have hair down there and I don't?") It is important that your child feels heard, and it is fine to tell them to save their potty questions for the bathroom. Try to be as honest as possible with your child, no matter what they are asking. Children often discover the differences between boy and girl parts during the potty training process, especially if both mom and dad are allowing the child into the bathroom for teaching purposes. If you can't answer a question or don't feel comfortable answering a specific question, try redirecting your child to a different topic or tell them that you need some time to think about their question before answering. Some parents try to limit the discussion of potty talk and questions to bathroom/potty time. Keeping potty words and potty talk in the bathroom (and redirecting all inappropriate talk to the bathroom) will help teach your child that pee and poop are not appropriate topics for dinnertime conversation. Of course, you and your partner should discuss the specific "rules" that will work best for your child and family.

BEST OF LUCK AND HAVE FUN!!

Well, now you have all the key information you need in order to undertake the potty training process with enthusiasm, confidence, and success!

Remember to stay positive and encouraging, and to be a cheerleader for your child as they undertake yet another developmental challenge and cross yet another developmental threshold.

Most importantly, pat yourself on the back for rising to the constant challenges of parenthood with grace and gumption!

9

Common Questions and Answers about Potty Training

Q: What is my role as a parent when potty training my child?

A: Your primary role as a parent is to support and encourage your child. You cannot force your child to potty train, as much as you may want them to. Your secondary role is to be a keen observer of your child's bodily cues and overall readiness for potty training. (See Chapter 3: *Is Your Child Ready? Are You?*, for a full discussion of the potty readiness issue.)

As a parent, remember to be positive and patient. As you know by now, you cannot insist that your child sit up, crawl, walk, or talk. Children simply do this when they are ready. It is the same for potty training, and your attitude during the potty training process sets the tone for your child. Allow your child to see that you are proud and supportive of their successes, and patient with their setbacks and accidents.

Q: How long will it take for my child to become fully potty trained?

A: The answer to this question depends on the child. Some children are able to potty train within a day. Most children, however, will need at least several weeks of consistent support, structure, and encouragement. Some children may take months or even a year or two before they are 100% potty trained. Whether your child potty trains on the short or long end of the spectrum is really up to them and your overall training process. There is no right or wrong time frame.

Q: Will potty training my son be different than potty training my daughter?

A: It is true that girls tend to mature at a somewhat faster rate than boys, particularly during the toddler years. On average, girls tend to potty train about three months earlier than boys.

As far as potty training itself, boys and girls should be taught in the same way. Both boys and girls should begin potty training while sitting down on the potty. To prevent spraying, boys may need to use the shield that comes with the potty chair, but can also be taught to point their penis down or to lean forward while peeing on the potty. After a boy has mastered both peeing and pooping on the potty and has been doing so for several months, you can begin introducing the concept of standing up to pee. Boys usually don't need any additional training to be able to pee into the toilet, but will need to be taught how to "aim" so that they don't spray all over the bathroom. There are many different ways to teach boys to aim, with the easiest (and cheapest) way being to put a piece of O-shaped cereal into the toilet so that the boy can aim at it. Another fun way to get your male child to pee in the toilet is to emphasize how the pee makes bubbles in the water!

> ### *Quick Tip: Sitting Down or Standing Up?*
> Both boys and girls should begin potty training while sitting down on the potty.

A very important point specific to training girls is to be sure that they are taught to wipe from front to back. Wiping from back to front will introduce bacteria into the urethra (the opening where the pee comes out) and can cause urinary tract infections.

Q: When should I teach my son to lift the toilet seat when he pees?

A: It is not essential to do this at the beginning of toilet training. Successfully using the potty chair for pee and poop is enough for most boys to master during the first few months of potty training. It is fine to teach them to lift the seat when they are older and have already mastered the key components of potty training. On the other hand, it can be beneficial to teach the complete toileting sequence from the beginning so that your son develops the "lifting the seat" habit from the start. Some children have a hard time when a routine is changed. Decide what works best for your child.

Q: What bathroom safety or hygiene issues I should be aware of?

A: Before you begin potty training, be sure your water heater is set to a maximum of 120 degrees Fahrenheit. This will prevent your young hand washer from being burned by hot water.

If your child is the curious type, you should invest in a toilet seat lock. These usually slip over the toilet seat cover and prevent little hands from being able to open them, but are easy enough for older children to be able to remove for using the toilet. This will keep your child out of the toilet and away from the water inside of it.

As with the rest of your house, any exposed outlets in the bathroom should have childproof caps that prevent children from being able to access them. You will also need to move any electrical appliances such as hair dryers, electric toothbrushes, or curling irons so that children cannot reach them. All of these appliances pose an electrocution hazard if they are used improperly, and should all be kept well out of your child's reach.

Q: My daughter started potty training and was excited to wear big kid underpants, but now she is asking for her diaper back. What should I do?

A: Setbacks can occur anytime during the training process and are to be expected. This is a time when being a good detective will help you. Have there been any major changes in your daughter's schedule or family life? These kinds of disruptions may make it hard for your child to move forward in her development at the moment. Major changes in a child's life, like starting a new school, getting a new caregiver, moving, or having a parent start a new job can set your child back for a brief time. If this is the case, be supportive and gentle with your child. Perhaps allow your child to use their diaper, but keep the big girl underpants out and visible and encourage your child to use them when she feels ready again. Continue the training process unless your child is distressed by it. If she is, then it might be time to take a break from training until your child shows signs of being ready again.

Parent Point-of-View

"When my daughter asked for her diaper back during potty training, I wanted to cry but my friend suggested that I just allow her the freedom to follow her instincts. So, I set out the diapers next to the underpants on her dresser. Each morning I said to her, 'You are doing so well using the potty, which of these do you want to wear today?' She picked the diaper and then I said, 'Ok. And when you are ready again, I know you will choose the underpants.' I remained positive and by the end of the week she was back in her Sleeping Beauty underwear!"

Q: Can I allow my older child to help with potty training?

A: Older siblings often enjoy helping with potty training. If they have a positive relationship with their younger sister or brother, they can be a motivating role model for your younger child. Be clear with your older child about the specific steps in your potty training process, and be there to supervise their help. Explain that it is OK if the younger sibling has an accident, or is not always successful. If this happens, teach your older child the specific words of encouragement to use, and also what to do with the soiled clothing. The bottom line is that younger siblings love to mimic their older counterparts, and training can go more smoothly and quickly with an older sibling's positive support.

Q: My son won't stop talking about peeing and pooping and his penis when we are in public. What should I do?

A: When children are potty training, it is typical for them to be excited to use their new terminology and it is important for them to do so. It is also important to set boundaries for talking about the potty, and a child's penis or vagina. One way to do this is to remind your child that "potty talk" only happens when using the potty or when you are at home. Also explain that if they feel the need to use potty talk in public, they can ask to talk to you privately.

It is essential to use a neutral tone of voice when reminding your child about "potty talk." If they sense that they can make you aggravated or embarrassed, they will be motivated to keep testing your boundaries. When they do restrain their potty talk to the proper setting, be sure to praise them or even give them a reward to reinforce their positive behavior.

"I made the understandable mistake of laughing hysterically when my son asked for a 'poopsicle' from the ice cream man. It caught me off guard and I couldn't help myself. However, he was so empowered by my reaction that he continued for weeks using the same line every time we went somewhere. I had to work very hard at simply reminding him that potty talk was only for the bathroom. When that didn't stop him, I actually decided to ignore his comments completely and changed the subject when he talked about 'poopsicles' in public—and that worked!"

Q: What is the typical age a child is ready to be potty trained?

A: The age when children are potty trained has steadily risen over the decades. In the 1940s, it was typical to begin potty training at eighteen months. Now, in the United States, girls begin potty training on average around thirty five months, and boys around 39 months, but every child is unique and should be potty trained when they show signs of being ready. See Chapter 3: *Is Your Child Ready? Are You?*, for how to assess your child's physical and emotional readiness for potty training.

Q: Will potty training affect my child's self-esteem?

A: Like every developmental milestone in a child's life, potty training presents the opportunity for emotional growth and increased self-esteem. That is why it is so important to praise and encourage your child throughout the process. This enables your child to be proud of their efforts and accomplishments and to see their accidents and mistakes as part of the journey.

Also, children become very proud of themselves when they learn a new task and can then do it independently. Potty training therefore offers parents an opportunity to build their child's positive self-esteem.

Q: Almost all my daughter's playmates are potty trained. Is it possible I have waited too long?

A: Rest assured your child will be potty trained. If you are paying attention to your child's individual readiness, then you have not waited too long. If you are concerned, you can begin to introduce potty books, DVDs, or dolls. Purchase a potty chair and simply leave it in the bathroom. Eventually your daughter will take an interest and you can embark on your potty training adventure together. Pushing your child before they are ready will likely backfire. Only you can decide if your child needs a gentle push, or just a little more time to be ready. See the Readiness Checklists in Chapter 1: *Quick Summaries to Get You Started*, to assess your child's physical and emotional readiness for potty train

---

Parent Point-of-View 🔍

"I knew my son wasn't ready to potty train, but I felt so much pressure from my friends to start that I forced the issue. I put up with tears, toilet paper strewn everywhere, and puddles of water from hand washing. It wasn't until my son peed all over his walls that I got the message: Do not force your child to potty train! If your friends pressure you, simply tell them that you respect your child's development and you'll train him when he is ready!"

Q: My son is showing every sign of being ready to potty train, but we are planning to move to a new state in two weeks. Should I start training now or wait until we have settled into our new home?

A: Potty training is a time of transition for children. They are moving from one developmental phase of their young lives to another. That is why potty training is best begun when things are relatively stable. It is likely that if you begin now, your son will have a setback during the move. It might be best not to start a formal training process at this time. If your son begins to use the potty spontaneously, then encourage his efforts. Otherwise, wait until you are settled into your new home to begin your training. You will likely have a smoother, more enjoyable experience with your child.

Q: When should I switch my child to actual underpants?

A: Generally, it is most effective to switch your child to underpants when they have begun to consistently use the potty to pee and poop. Accidents will occur as the training process moves along, and moving into underpants too soon can be messy and discouraging to your child.

However, some children may be motivated by the idea of big kid underwear. If your child is insisting on using underpants but is not quite ready, you can allow them to wear underpants at home where accidents are easier to handle and let them wear pull-ups or diapers when you are out. You can decide what works best for your child.

Q: What are some good ways to prepare my child for potty training, even before they are ready to sit on the potty?

A: One good way to begin is to start giving your child simple instructions for simple tasks and help them carry them out. For example, when it is time to clean up their toys, give directions: "It is time to clean up your toys. First, put the books on the shelf. Second, put the blocks in the bin. Then put the bin on the shelf." Make the instructions simple and clear, and then praise and support their efforts. By practicing following directions, they will learn to be more independent and self sufficient. These are skills they will need for potty training as well. You can use other simple tasks to practice, like setting out their clothes for the next day, putting a cup in the dishwasher, or putting on their coat. Be sure to praise their efforts and encourage them to try to do things on their own as much as possible.

As we discussed earlier in this book, there are other things you can do to prepare your child. Narrate diaper changes, explaining what you are doing and why. Show your child their dirty diaper and explain how big kids and grown-ups poop and pee on the potty instead of in a diaper. You can also practice flushing poop from a diaper down the toilet. And, if you are comfortable, bring your child into the bathroom with you and explain what you are doing when you use the toilet. All these things can prepare your child for their own adventure with potty training. See Chapter 5: *Pre-Potty Training with Your Child*, for detailed information on pre-potty training.

Q: One day I went into the playroom and my son had taken off his poopy diaper and smeared the poop all over the walls. I was horrified but tried not to show it. Is this normal?

A: Children learn about their world through exploration. Although the idea of poop-smeared walls is revolting to adults, your child is simply expressing his curiosity about poop. It is important in this circumstance not to yell or become angry. This will likely confuse your child and could lead to poor self-esteem and more serious issues around bowel elimination. Instead, use the opportunity to talk about what poop is, where it comes from, and what happens to it when you are a big kid or grown-up. Use a neutral voice and explain that poop stays in a diaper or in a toilet and nowhere else. If you haven't already, this would be a good time to introduce books or DVDs about poop and about using the potty as well.

Q: What do I do when we go on vacation? We just started potty training and I don't want an accident in the car.

A: There are a few options when traveling with a child who is in the midst of potty training. The first is to use pull-ups or diapers in the car, and stop frequently for bathroom breaks. You can also cover the car seat and limit fluid intake. You may also want to bring your potty chair or toilet topper with you and use it at a rest stop if your child is comfortable doing so. Also, dress your child in clothes that can be removed quickly so that you have the best chance of making it to a potty without an accident.

When you are traveling, it is important to remain as consistent as possible with the potty training routine you have already established. Bring your reward or sticker chart with you, as well as your potty books and DVDs if your child uses them. Remember to praise your child's successes and reassure them that it is OK if they have an accident.

Parent Point-of-View
"We have twins—a boy and a girl—and had to develop a 'two potty system' for traveling. We let each child choose whether they wanted to bring their potty chair or toilet topper. Our daughter also wanted to have Cheerios to pee on like her brother, and our son wanted to go into the ladies room with my wife. We let the kids choose and it made the entire trip more enjoyable and I have to say— accident free!"

Q: After using the potty, my child uses hand washing time as play time. She splashes and makes an incredible mess. What can I do to stop this?

A: Your child may be letting off steam after her success with the potty, or she may just think that hand washing is the same as bath time. Explain the potty training steps again. Focus specifically on hand washing and explain why it is not a time to splash and be silly. Let your child know that if she can wash her hands correctly, she may choose any hand soap that she wants from the store. There are a variety of fun soaps to choose from, and this will likely motivate your child to follow the hand washing rules. You can also purchase a special towel just for your child, or add hand washing to your sticker chart and reward her when she washes them appropriately.

Q: My son pees on the potty very consistently, but still asks to wear a pull-up when he needs to poop. Should I force him to use the potty, or give him the pull-up?

A: Your son is expressing his current needs. He is not yet ready to poop in the potty, so giving him the pull-up is a positive and respectful thing to do. When you give him the pull-up, let him know that you understand he is not yet ready to poop in the potty, but that he should tell you when he is ready. If you try to force him to use the potty, it will likely create a struggle and negative associations about pooping in general. Continue to be supportive and patient, and know that one day he will indeed be ready to poop in the potty.

Q: I started potty training my son and I don't think he is ready. Should I stop, or keep pushing the issue?

A: It is common for parents to begin potty training only to find out that their child is resistant or outright defiant about the process. If this is the case, it is best to respect your child's development and halt the training until your child is ready. Simply say "I know you will be ready soon, and when you are we will try again." This will give your child relief and a sense of well being because you have honored his process. You will also save yourself hours of frustration and power struggles that could lead to a strained relationship with your child. Remember, you can't force your child to be potty trained any more than you can force him to start walking. See Chapter 3: *Is Your Child Ready? Are You?*, for more information about physical and emotional readiness for potty training.

Parent Point-of-View

"My daughter was peeing on the potty, but not pooping. She used one particular corner of the living room to retreat to when she wanted to poop in her diaper. I decided to encourage her awareness of needing to poop by saying 'Shelly is my girl on the go,' whenever she retreated. She loved it and after about a week she came up to me and said, "Mommy, I'm a girl on the go," and went into the bathroom and pooped on the potty!"

Q: My new caregiver is not following the potty training protocol that my husband and I have set in motion. Is this a problem?

A: Consistency is essential for children, and that is especially true for potty training as well. It is important for your caregiver to be a core member of the potty training team. Next time she is scheduled to come, spend some time with her explaining your process and why you need her to stay on the same page. Be sure to ask if she has any questions about the process, including the reward system and the language you have chosen to use with your child. If possible, go through a potty session with both your caregiver and child present to be sure that they are both comfortable.

Q: Isn't using a reward system for potty training simply bribing my child? I'm afraid if I bribe him he won't learn to use the potty of his own accord.

A: There is a tremendous difference between using a reward system and bribing a child. A reward system enables a child to strive toward a specific goal and be rewarded when it is met. Something like a sticker chart helps both you and your child chart the progress and accomplishments in potty training, which is very motivating for children. When a goal is met and rewarded, the positive behavior is reinforced. This encourages a child to be proud of their efforts and continue to strive forward.

Alternatively, a bribe is a short term, immediate response to forcing your child into a behavior you want in the moment. Most parents have resorted to bribery at one time or another, and know that it does not promote long term behavior change.

For example, if your child is having a meltdown in the grocery store and you tell them that they can get a toy if they stop, they will stop—but only in that one moment. Next time you go to a grocery store, your child will likely cry again because last time he did this you gave him a toy. Bribery will not change behavior. Using a reward system that charts specific goals and rewards a child only when those goals are met will reinforce the positive behavior you are seeking.

Q: Is it okay to let my son pee outside if it is an emergency?

A: During the potty training process, you will likely find yourself in a situation where your child needs to pee and there is no restroom available. In this case, you have two choices: an accident, or finding a discreet way to allow your child to pee outside. The latter is often the better choice and should be accompanied by an explanation that peeing outside is *only* done in an emergency. Tell your child that they should continue to try to use a toilet when they need to pee so they do not begin to rely on going outside. Also, if you know that you will be going to a park or other outdoor space without a restroom, encourage your child to use the potty before you go.

Q: My daughter has been potty trained for months and suddenly she had an accident. Should I be concerned?

A: Accidents are to be expected along the potty training road. Many children who are fully potty trained have temporary setbacks or accidents. There is no need to be alarmed. Simply continue to be supportive and encouraging of your child's ability to use the potty. By all means, do not make a big fuss over the incident.

If the accidents continue or become frequent, do some detective work regarding your child's current home and school environment. Has any major transition or schedule change occurred? Is your child having difficulty at school or with another child? Has there been a death in the family or other major family change? If you continue to be concerned, talk to your caregiver or your child's teacher. If you cannot find any environmental reason for a setback and are still concerned, talk to your pediatrician.

Q: I find myself getting so frustrated with the whole potty training process. My child sits forever on the potty and does nothing. How can I be more patient?

A: Most parents become frustrated and impatient at some time during the potty training process. We all lead busy lives and the idea of sitting in the bathroom reading books and talking about poop and pee when there is dinner to prepare and work to be done can be maddening. However, it may help to remember that this process is a temporary one. As your child progresses, he will spend less time in the bathroom and eventually use the toilet like everyone else. You will not have to spend the rest of your life talking about poop and pee!

Potty training is a time when children move from using a diaper to recognizing their own bodily signals for elimination. It is a time of tremendous transition for children, and your attitude as a parent is so important. Remind yourself that it is in your child's best interest for you to remain calm, patient, and supportive. It may also help to talk to other parents who are going through potty training as they are likely experiencing the same feelings that you are. You can also make a Potty Training Patience Plan for yourself. See Chapter 6: *Potty Training: Nuts and Bolts!*, for further details on this helpful strategy.

Q: I'd like to get two potties—one for the bathroom and one for the playroom to avoid accidents on the way to the bathroom. Is that an appropriate thing to do?

A: It is really a matter of choice. It is common for children to be so engrossed in play that they wait too long to use the potty. In order to avoid too many accidents in the beginning, it may be useful to have a potty chair where your child plays. Be sure to put a plastic liner underneath the chair and designate a specific area for it. Eventually you may find it beneficial to tell your child that they are doing so well, they no longer need a potty in the playroom. Praise them for their progress and let them know that from now on all peeing and pooping will happen in the bathroom.

Q: Should I expect my child to pee or poop in the potty right away?

A: As we explain in this book, it is a good idea to have your child first practice sitting on the potty without any expectation of making a poop or pee. This is a good way to help your child become comfortable with the potty training process without any pressure. Be sure to remove their diaper before beginning, and wash their hands when they are all done sitting on the potty. This way you can establish your routine from the beginning. When your child is ready to actually use the potty, they will be comfortable with what to do. See Chapter 5: *Pre-Potty Training with Your Child*, for other pre-potty training strategies that will help your child.

Q: Whenever I ask my child if she needs to go to the potty, she says "no" and it almost always results in an accident. What can I do?

A: If you see signals that your child needs to use the potty, it is important that you don't ask them if they need to go, but that you TELL them. This way you are helping your child recognize their own bodily signals for needing to use the toilet.

For example, if you see your son crossing his legs and wiggling in his seat, you can say, "I see that you are crossing your legs and wiggling. You need to use the potty." If he says no, gently usher him to the bathroom and have him try. He may be surprised at first with your accuracy, but eventually he will accept his own signals and be proud to pay attention to them.

Q: I am feeling a lot of pressure from my family and some friends to start potty training my child—even though I know she is not ready. Should I begin the process, or not?

A: Although it can be difficult, it is essential to ignore competitive or pushy family and friends. Although they may be well meaning, no one knows your child better than you do. As a parent, it is your responsibility to do what is best for your child. By giving your child time and space to potty train on their own timetable, you show them respect as an individual and lay important groundwork for a healthy parent-child relationship.

When it comes to handling pressure from friends and family, simply say, "Thank you so much for your input, but I am following the advice of our pediatrician." Then, change the subject and continue to honor your child's individual development.

Q: How can I avoid power struggles with my son over the potty training process?

A: If you are having frequent power struggles over potty training, it may be that your child is not quite ready to begin the process. It is important to step back at this point and allow your child more time. Rushing or pushing your child before they are ready can lead to frustration and conflict.

If you believe your child is ready and perhaps the power struggle is due to temperament, it may help to give your child some control or choices where possible. For example, you can let your child choose the type of sticker they want to earn, what kind of underpants to wear, or where to put the potty in the bathroom. You can say things like, "Great job! You earned a sticker on your chart. Would you like to put it on, or should I? Would you like chicken for dinner, or a hot dog? Do you want to go to the rose garden park or the dog park?" Simple gestures like offering two clear choices can help your child feel in control and independent, and also ease power struggles.

Q: Things have gone great with our potty training, and my son hasn't had an accident for four months. Are we officially finished with potty training?

A: Potty training will continue for some time, even after your child is competent using the toilet. You will still monitor your child's potty needs, and remain aware of bathroom breaks, potty signals, and available toilets when out and about with your child. Likely you will still need to give your child reminders and continue to ask if they need to use the potty. After all, children who are potty trained can still have accidents when they are in a new environment, experience a life transition, or simply become too engrossed in play.

It is a good idea to keep a full change of clothes with you on play dates, park outings, and when traveling. Many preschools and kindergartens also require that a full change of clothes be kept at school. If an accident occurs, it is still important to treat your child with patience and respect, and let them know accidents can happen and it is okay.

Q: My daughter is fully potty trained during the day, but still sleeps in a pull-up at night and is always wet in the morning. Is this a problem?

A: It is not uncommon for children to be potty trained during the day, but still wet the bed at night. Experts are not sure why, but likely it is due to a child's overall development. Some children are not developmentally ready to know that their bladder is full and they need to wake up. Others may not have developed enough bladder control, or may simply sleep so soundly they do not sense the need to pee and sleep through the signals. Generally, when your child's body is developed enough they will be dry at night or wake to pee. However, if you have concerns regarding your child's bed wetting, be sure to contact your pediatrician.

Q: My son is eight years old and still wets the bed. My pediatrician suggests that we use an alarm system designed to train our child to wake up and pee. Do these systems really work?

A: There are a variety of effective alarm systems you can purchase to help your child learn to wake when they need to pee. Generally, these systems utilize specially designed underpants or bed pads that are highly sensitive to moisture; an alarm is triggered when the first signs of pee are detected. The systems also come with specific instructions on what to do with your child when the alarm sounds. This includes fully waking your child, having them turn off the alarm and walking them to the toilet to pee even if they have already eliminated their urine in bed. Many systems also come with a chart and stickers to track your child's progress and help motivate them.

The key to using these systems is consistency and commitment. In the beginning, waking to an alarm in the middle of the night is jarring and exhausting for both parent and child. If you can, start using the alarm system during a school vacation or other time period that is less taxing for everyone and will not include travel or major life transitions. Depending on your child, it can take between two and six months until they are fully trained.

Parent Point-of-View

"We purchased a wireless alarm system for our nine-year-old son which worked except for the fact that our son was such a heavy sleeper he never woke up to the alarm—only we did! We decided to purchase an accessory that was basically a vibrating disc that went under his pillow. When the alarm sounded the disc vibrated like an earthquake and woke him up. Once we did this, it only took three weeks for him to overcome his bed-wetting."

Q: When can I remove the potty chair and other potty toys from the bathroom?

A: Once a child is using the toilet consistently, most parents can't wait until their bathroom is once again potty free. However, this is a time to be attentive to and respectful of your child's temperament, and to be sensitive to their particular feelings about change. Some children won't care at all if you remove all the books, toys, and the potty chair. Other children who are more sensitive to change will need transition time to let go of all their potty props. Monitor your child's needs and respond in a loving and patient way.

Q: Do I need to talk to my doctor before I begin potty training, or any time during the process?

A: Potty training issues do not usually require the assistance of a doctor, but you should feel free to call if you have a health concern. If your child is still not potty trained by the time they begin kindergarten, this may warrant a call or visit to the pediatrician. Nighttime incontinence after age nine is another issue that a doctor needs to assess, and may need to be treated with medication.

   If your child complains of pain or burning during urination, this is a likely sign of a urinary tract infection and you should call the doctor. Complaints of abdominal pain should also be monitored, and you should call the doctor if the abdominal pain (tummy ache) persists or is accompanied by a fever. If you notice your child is leaking stool and does not notice, this is a sign of encopresis, or severe constipation, and your child should be examined by a physician.

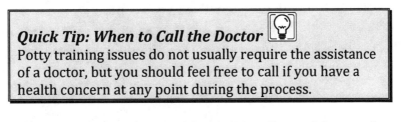

Quick Tip: When to Call the Doctor
Potty training issues do not usually require the assistance of a doctor, but you should feel free to call if you have a health concern at any point during the process.

Q: Is it important to have a "Potty Party" to celebrate after our child is fully potty trained?

A: Celebrating any major achievement during your child's life can be a way to reinforce their self-esteem and let them know you are proud of them and that they can be proud of themselves. This can be as simple as making a special dinner, or taking time to talk with your child about where they started in the process and what they did to accomplish their goal.

Some parents enjoy having a mini-party with balloons and cake, going to dinner, or even having an actual party with family and friends. The important thing is to take the time to acknowledge this major milestone in your child's development in a positive, affirming way.

> **Parent Point-of-View**
> "After each of our children were potty trained, my husband and I had a cake made that said 'Way To Go!" and had a miniature plastic toilet on top. Both of the kids loved it and our son still has the mini-toilet on his shelf! Don't be afraid to make the process fun!"

We now bid you farewell as you embark on your own exciting potty training adventure. Hopefully you have found this guide informative and inspiring. As you close this book, we hope you will always remember to approach potty training with patience and love. Try to be creative and accommodate your little one as much as possible. Rest assured, all children learn to use the toilet eventually and your child will certainly not be the exception.

Have some fun with it! Good luck!

More Great Books from the *What Now?* Series!

Lesson Ladder is dedicated to helping you prepare for life's most fundamental challenges. We provide practical tools and well-rounded advice that help you achieve your goals while climbing the personal or professional ladder—whether it is preparing to start a family of your own, getting your child potty trained, or learning a new kind of financial management.

Companion Books for the Little One

Sophie's Magic Underwear

This colorful and playful book
encompasses the journey of
Sophie– a toddler turned voice of
reason– who speaks to the reader
about how her magic underwear
keep her from going to the
bathroom in her pants. The book helps bring light to what can
sometimes be a difficult topic for parents through the use of
magic and Sophie's cheerful friend Bunny.
978-0-98486-570-3 | $7.95

Sammy's Super-Powered Underwear

Follow Sammy and his friend
Super Bear through a journey of
how his super-powered
underwear keeps him from going
to the bathroom in his pants. With
a little pep in his step, Sammy
teaches the importance of
understanding the setbacks of
accidents but also in moving forward through putting on
another pair of super-powered underwear – and realizing that
the real super power lies inside of you – the reader.
978-0-9848657-5-8 | $7.99

Call toll-free to order! 1-800-301-4647
Or order online: www.LessonLadder.com

ABOUT THE AUTHOR

After becoming a mother of two children and potty training her young son, Dr. Patricia Wynne realized that toilet training was a dynamic and highly individualized process. Despite making many mistakes herself, her son was successfully potty trained by the age of 2 1/2. At the end of her tumultuous journey, she felt inspired to write this book and share what she had learned with other parents. She now spends her time writing about parenting and caring for her two young children who are both under the age of 3.

Prior to motherhood, Dr. Wynne obtained her doctorate degree in Neuroscience from the University of Massachusetts Medical School. Her diverse passions include researching the molecular underpinnings of alcoholism, business development in the biotechnology sector, intellectual property law, and teaching. As a result of her multi-faceted interests, Dr. Wynne has also earned her M.B.A. from the University of Massachusetts, Isenberg School of Management, and is a registered patent agent with the United States Patent and Trademark Office. She has been published in journals such as *Neuron*, the *Journal of Neuroscience*, and the *Journal of Pharmacology and Experimental Therapeutics*.

For a more behind-the-scenes look at Dr. Wynne's own personal potty training experience and other parenting tips, please visit her blog which can be found at www.lessonladder.com.

CPSIA information can be obtained at www.ICGtesting.com
Printed in the USA
BVOW07s0856250913

332115BV00005B/11/P